YOU'RE BETTER THAN YOUR JOB SEARCH

MARC CENEDELLA AND **MATTHEW ROTHENBERG**

WWW.THELADDERS.COM

The Ladders®

Marc Cenedella: Founder and CEO
Matthew Rothenberg: Director, Editorial and Content
Lou Casale: Vice President of Corporate Communications
John Hazard: News Editor
Susan Conroy: Managing Editor
Andrew Klappholz: Fact Checker
Dara Cothran: Manager, Public Relations
Tarmi Addonizio: In-house Counsel

DOWNTOWN BOOKWORKS INC.

Produced by Downtown Bookworks Inc.

Designed by Priest + Grace

ISBN: 978-1-935703-10-5

To order copies of this book visit us at www.theLadders.com.

We welcome your comments and suggestions. Please write to us at matthewr@theladders.com.

10 9 8 7 6 5 4 3 2 1

To the people of TheLadders ...
The brighter the students, the more the
teacher learns ...

Love & win,
Marc

III

Acknowledgments

This book is built on centuries of aggregate experience our expert sources have shared about every phase of the job search. Here's a list of professionals whose generosity, patience and expertise allowed us to tell this tale. (Many of them are authors in their own right, and we encourage you to explore their insights in the works cited below.)

Sharon Reed Abboud *Author of "All Moms Work: Short-Term Career Strategies for Long-Range Success"*

Greg Bennett *Recruiter at the Mergis Group in Raleigh, N.C.*

Jodie Bentley *CEO and co-founder of The Savvy Actor Inc.*

Christine Bolzan *CEO of Graduate Career Coaching*

Jim Brown *President of Jim Brown Associates in San Francisco*

Deborah Brown-Volkman *Professional certified coach and president of a career, life and mentor coaching company*

Steve Burdan *Certified professional resume writer with TheLadders*

Robert E. Capwell *Chief knowledge officer at Employment Background Investigations*

Dr. Marlene Caroselli *Corporate trainer and author of dozens of management books*

Clark Christensen *Currently with the corporate finance function of Coca-Cola, responsible for financial analysis; former CFO of PS Energy Group Inc. in Atlanta*

Brian Clark *Director of business development for Answer Financial*

Roy Cohen *Master career coach at the Five O'Clock Club*

Amanda Collins *Chief of staff at The Grammar Doctors*

Tony Deblauwe *Founder of HR4Change*

Douglas Dickerman *Actor*

Kelly Dingee *Sourcing researcher and trainer at AIRS*

David A. Earle *Managing partner at Staffing.org*

Jay Edelman *President of Top 5 Data Services*

John Treacy Egan *Star of "The Producers" and "The Little Mermaid"*

Raoul Encinas *Board member of the Scottsdale Job Network and vice president of Preod, a professional services firm based in Princeton, N.J.*

Chris Forman *Former president of AIRS*

Kathryn J. Fraser *Psychiatrist and associate professor of psychiatry at U. of New Mexico School of Medicine in Albuquerque*

David Freeman *Consultant at Sonic Recruit, a division of Cytiva Software Inc.*

Aliza Freud *CEO of SheSpeaks.com*

Elizabeth Friedman *Clinical psychologist in New York*

Paul Gillin *Head of Paul Gillin Communications and author of "The New Influencers: A Marketer's Guide to the New Social Media"*

Natalie Goldberg *Author of "Writing Down the Bones: Freeing the Writer Within"*

Samantha Goldberg *Celebrity event designer and TV personality*

Randy Hain *Managing partner at Bell Oaks Executive Search in Atlanta*

Sally Haver *Senior vice president of business development at The Ayers Group/Career Partners International*

Robert Hawthorne *President of Hawthorne Executive Search*

Deidre Henry *Television and film actress*

Michael Hickins *News editor at The Wall Street Journal*

Isabel Walcott Hilborn *Owner of Strategic Internet Consulting and founder, SmartGirl.com*

Shel Horowitz *Marketing consultant and "ethical marketing expert"*

Jacqueline Hudson *Senior account executive for the Renascent Group LLC*

Rick Joers *Currently head of policy and employment–Americas, The Royal Bank of Scotland; formerly vice president of human resources at JP Morgan*

Michael Jolkovski *Psychologist and psychoanalyst in Falls Church, Va.; principal at Working Through, a consultancy focused on helping creative teams*

Josh Klenoff *President of JKCoaching.com*

Dan Kohrman *Senior attorney at AARP overseeing age-discrimination cases*

Abby Kohut *President of Staffing Symphony and head of AbsolutelyAbby.com*

Larry Lambeth *President of Employment Screening Services Inc.*

Harold Laslo *Currently chief recruiter/principle of Hlaslo & Associates Group Inc.; formerly of The Aldan Troy Group in New York*

Frank Laux *President of Strategic Search Partners in Keller, Texas*

Bruce Lee *Spokesman for Mercer, a global human resources and financial-consulting company*

David Lewis *Author of "The Emerging Leader: Eight Lessons for Life in Leadership"*

Charlene Li *President of the Altimeter Group*

Kate Lukach *Director of marketing for SelectMinds, a software provider*

Barry Maher *Business speaker*

Angie Maizlish *President of First Impressions and a certified professional resume writer and certified employment interview professional*

Irene Marshall *MBA, PhD, certified resume writer, career coach and interview coach*

Thomas G. Martin *President of Martin Investigative Services in Newport Beach, Calif.*

Linda Matias *Author of "201 Knock-out Answers to Tough Interview Questions: The Ultimate Guide to Handling the New Competency-Based Interview Style"*

Ed McGlynn *President of Financial Recruiters LLC*

Carol Meerschaert *Director of marketing and communications for the Healthcare Businesswomen's Association*

Laura Michnya *Project manager of recruiting systems and process for BAE Systems*

Michael Neece *Chief strategy officer of PongoResume and InterviewMastery.com*

Robert Neelbauer *Owner of StaffMagnet.com*

Colleen O'Neill *Senior partner and principal at Mercer*

Lindsay Olson *Partner and recruiter at Paradigm Staffing*

Cheryl Palmer *President of CalltoCareer.com*

Deidre Pannazzo *Executive director at Inspired Resumes*

Ronald Parks *Managing director at eConsult America in Minneapolis*

Marlane Perry *Managing director of the executive search division of Magill Associates*

Katy Piotrowski *Career Solutions Group*

Jo Prabhu *Founder and CEO of placement firm 1800Jobquest, Long Beach, Calif.*

Victoria Pynchon *Mediator at ADR Services*

Lisa Quast *President and founder of Career Woman Inc. and a certified executive coach and author*

Ellen Gordon Reeves *Author of "Can I Wear My Nose Ring to the Interview?"*

Susan Reinhard *Senior vice president of the AARP Public Policy Institute*

Kelley Rexroad *Founder of KREX Consulting*

Rachel Rice-Haase *SPHR; Human resources and marketing coordinator for Oberstadt Landscapes & Nursery, Inc.*

Marian Rich *Recruiter with Bonell Ryan search firm in New York*

Frank Risalvato *President of IRESInc., an executive search firm specializing in insurance and financial services*

Art Romero *Managing director of Academy Recruiting in Denver*

Les Rosen *President of Employment Screening Resources, www.ESRcheck.com; founding member of the National Association of Professional Background Screeners; and former California deputy district attorney*

Matthew Rosen *Vice president of human resources for an Ohio-based manufacturing facility*

Michael Rosenberg *Manager of sales, productivity and performance at TheLadders*

Robert J. Rosenthal *Director of communications at VolunteerMatch.org*

Lisa Rowan *Program director of human resources*

Cindy Schneider *Currently with KRFC radio station; former corporate recruiting consultant at Intuit in Fort Collins, Colo.*

Stephen Seckler *President of Seckler Legal Coaching*

Jeremy Shapiro *Senior vice president of Hodes iQ*

Matt Sigelman *CEO of Burning Glass*

Kevin Skinner *Marriage and family therapist and writer for MyExpertSolution.com*

Ed Sordellini *Executive recruiter in Wilmington, N.C.*

Donna Spellman *Director of Self-Sufficiency Services at Family Centers of Greenwich, Conn.*

Rick Stomphorst *Econstruction.com*

Theo Stripling *Program associate with Literacy Volunteers of Illinois*

James Thompson *Vice president of business development for JMJ Phillip*

Justin Tobin *Psychotherapist in Chicago*

Stephen Van Vreede *Resume writer for TheLadders*

Ellen B. Vance *Former human resources consultant and auditor with Titan Group in Richmond, Va.*

Jim Villwock *Founder of Job Doctors International*

Laura Warren *Consultant and former California lobbyist*

Lynne Waymon *Author/co-founder of consultancy Contacts Count*

Jenny Yang *Former manager of product marketing for data-loss prevention at Symantec*

Rahul D. Yodh *Executive recruiter with Link Legal Search Group in Dallas*

Jillian Zavitz *Programs manager for TalktoCanada.com*

CONTENTS

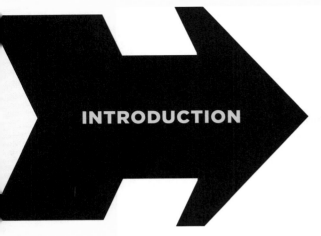

INTRODUCTION

It all went so wrong—so very, very wrong—right from the start.

You left your notepad with your handwritten questions at home; your CEO pulled you into a last-second meeting that made you a half-hour late to the interview; and you finished it off by saying "I think my background and experience make me uniquely suited to making a big contribution here at Avis," which was a good point ... except you were interviewing at Enterprise.

Whew. You had a bad day in the job hunt. A really bad one. You feel embarrassed, and you're starting to wonder if anybody is ever going to be foolish enough to hire you.

It happens to all of us. My job here at TheLadders is the 27th job that I've had in my life—from waiting tables so I could pay my way through college to SVP, Finance & Operations at HotJobs.com.

So I've been through 27 job hunts, and I could spend a couple of hours over lunch filling you in on all the stupid mistakes I've made.

I know what it's like to completely and utterly bomb the interview—the humiliation and the self-doubt and the worry that you're never going to find a new job because maybe, just maybe, you don't really deserve one.

And I know the anxiety that causes you to question yourself and feel like the whole system is set up to frustrate and defeat you. I'd like to tell you that it's easy to just brush it off and get back up and get going again. But it's not.

Because while goof-ups are a natural part of the process any time we're trying to do something new—a new golf swing, a new sport or finding a new job—and we should just take them in stride, that's one of those things that is easier said than done.

In the job hunt, we feel that too much is at stake, there's too much on the line, for us to just shake it off. And that's the problem.

You know, here at TheLadders, we spend a lot of time and effort studying the best ways to help you get into your next job as quickly and painlessly as possible. And one of the first things we've discovered is this sad fact:

The day after a "bad" day, the average job seeker only does half as much for his job hunt as he normally does. He only sends out half as many resumes, makes half as many calls and does half as much research. It's understandable. You're embarrassed, you're feeling foolish, you're having doubts about your abilities. All because of that bad day.

Shakespeare, as usual, may have said it best:

"Our doubts are traitors, and make us lose the good we oft might win, by fearing to attempt."

Our doubts are traitors, indeed. They sit there on your shoulder, bend your ear and whisper negative thoughts into your head. Which is a shame, because that same research shows there is a direct correlation between activity in the job hunt and finding your next job. So in a way, the little buggers whispering negative things in your ear are directly undermining your chances of success. Of course, when you sit back to think about it, this reduction in activity the day after a bad day is 180 degrees from the advice you'd give to somebody you care about when they are facing a similar situation.

The day after your daughter falls off her bike while she's learning to ride without training wheels, you don't tell her to try only half as hard today. And when your college buddy, who needs to drop more than a few pounds, blows his diet at Outback Steakhouse with the Bloomin' Onion, the 22-ounce Melbourne Steak and that dang delicious Chocolate Thunder from Down Under, you don't tell him it's OK to only try half as hard to stick to the diet today.

No, you tell the people you care about that the past is the past, and today is a new day and they should do something new with it. So here's the good news: While the average job seeker only puts half as much effort into his job hunt the day after a bad day, it's important for you to remember, you're not the average job seeker.

As somebody earning at the $100K+ level, you're in the top 10 percent of the American workforce and the top 1 percent globally. You got here because you're effective at dealing with business problems, and you've shown the leadership and management ability to overcome tough situations.

It's often said that finding a job is a job in itself. If that's the case, why shouldn't you treat a bad day on the job hunt the way you'd treat a bad day at the office? When the big sale is slipping away, or the budget is late, or the database crashed, or the agency hasn't turned around the work on time, you don't sit back. You leap into action.

And that sense of competence in overcoming the day-to-day problems of your job is the same sense of capability and effectiveness I'd like to ask you to bring to your job hunt.

The average job seeker only puts half as much effort into the job hunt the day after a bad interview.

The day after a bad day, especially the day after you've really, totally, completely blown it, treat it just like you would any challenge you face in business. Don't cut your effort in half ... double it.

You are in the top 10 percent for a reason, and that is because when all of the people in the country were put on a scale, you were found to be one of the best: the best at your job, the best at your business and the best at making yourself a success.

Matthew Rothenberg, Editor-in-Chief of TheLadders, and I have compiled and curated this book from the best career advice our team has gleaned about every step of the job search. We know from our experience that with the advice and tools we've developed, you will find your next great role in life. Sometimes the road is long and winding and twisted, and the destination feels like it is forever just out of sight. But from watching literally millions of your fellow job seekers, I can tell you that you, too, will find yours.

I'll be rooting for you.

— *Marc Cenedella*

Every job search tells a story, and each of those searches is a chapter in the narrative of a career. I've got a story; you've got a story; and millions of your fellow senior job seekers have stories of challenges, frustrations and triumphs.

TheLadders' editorial team is here to write, of course; we look to provide tactical guidance. But we're also here to listen to the real experts: job seekers like you, who've tackled nearly every ordinary situation and impossible scenario imaginable on the job search and come out on top.

Our readers are among the most seasoned and resourceful career managers on the planet. Their stories—specifically, their tools and tricks to advance their careers in myriad industries and functions across the country—provide unrivaled real-world models for how to conduct your own career. (And they also make great reading!)

This book synthesizes the research and writing of many talented journalists, including Elizabeth Bennett, Debra Donston-Miller, Kevin Fogarty, John Hazard, Joyann King, Nina Myers, Patty Orsini, Karl Rozemeyer, Donald Sears, Darryl Taft and Lisa Vaas.

Thanks to writers and readers alike for their talent and time.

— Matthew Rothenberg

START YOU

SEAR

TING
R
JOB
CH

IS IT YOUR AGE OR YOUR SALARY?

NETWORKING:
TALKING TO FRIENDS—AND COMPETITORS

HONING YOUR ELEVATOR PITCH

CREATE YOUR BRAND

RESUME WRITING
& PRESENTATION

HOW TO DEFINE YOUR JOB GOALS

You've made the decision that it's time to move on—or perhaps had the decision made for you—and your biggest question is, "How long is this going to take?"

The reality is, "Longer than you'd like." But the good news is that we can help.

You know, the first time you were invited to play golf, or went fly-fishing, or tried your hand at cooking a new cuisine, you didn't just grab the equipment and start slashing around the golf course, the river, or the kitchen. You took a bit of time to get to know the tools and the rules, and you got better as you went along.

Parts of the process of the job search may have changed since the last time you were in front of the desk. So before you jump the gun and start applying for jobs, writing up a resume and networking, take a little time to read this book. We've laid out a clear set of best practices you can use as a guide to keep your search on track and successful. You've done it before and come out well.

What you'll need to do first is define what you want from your job search and create an "elevator pitch" that explains those goals succinctly. Read on and we'll tell you how.

How to Define Your Job Goals

AT THIS SENIOR STAGE of your career, any job decision involves two key questions:
- What is it you hope to achieve next?
- What are you willing to do to get there?

Perhaps you want to earn more money, enjoy better job security or have more time to spend with your family. In exchange, you may be willing to consider greater or smaller changes to your current situation—and more or less effort to get there.

A simple move from one company to another in the same industry may require little disruption to your established routine. On the other hand, a bigger jump will demand more effort: You may need to change your industry, your location, your field or function, or other aspects of your career as you've experienced it thus far. It may even require sacrifices such as a lower salary to break into a healthier industry.

Think through what you're looking to change and what you're looking to keep the same, and check those items you're willing to change:

- ○ Company
- ○ Function
- ○ Industry
- ○ Location
- ○ Size of company (Fortune 1000 vs. start-up)
- ○ Compensation

How Long Will It Take?

AS A GENERAL RULE OF THUMB, your $100K+ job search will take five months plus one month for each box you've checked. Looking to move from the controller role in the consumer division to a similar role at the same company in the enterprise division? Plan on five months.

Looking to change companies but remain in your field and industry? That should take about six.

Looking to move from your big corporate multinational to a start-up across the country? Expect it to take seven.

Been running your own consulting business for the past decade and want to move to work for a client? That's eight. (Because you're changing your company, your size and your function—switching from being the executive to being an employee is a function.)

Once you've figured out what you'd like to do, you'll need to explain it to others.

While you are well aware of how accomplished you are, your future boss isn't yet. And you'll need to have a brief—very brief—way of explaining to anybody you happen to meet what you'd like to do.

Honing Your Elevator Pitch

WHETHER YOU'RE NETWORKING, talking to recruiters or at your 20-year college reunion chatting up old buddies, you'll need to explain your goals in 30 seconds or less, keep it positive and be specific without being boring.

As a matter of fact, that's why it's called an "elevator pitch." Because everybody is so busy these days, you need to be able to explain what you want to do, why you'll be good at it, and how they can help, in the time it takes for an elevator to go between floors in a building.

What are some examples of the right way and wrong way to create an elevator pitch?

Wrong

- "Oh, I'm looking to do anything in sales."

- "You know, with everything that's happened, I think it's time to get out of the derivatives industry, so I'm hoping to find somebody else that wants a guy with a decade of finance experience and a Wharton MBA."

- "They hired a new boss for my division and, boy, is he a bear. I really need to get away from working with such a negative person."

- "Oh, I don't know, it's just such a topsy-turvy time right now and I'm not sure what I should do next, it's so confusing because every time you think a company is stable and secure, poof!, some accounting scandal turns up and they go under, and I'm just so worried about making a choice that's going to turn out wrong, but I need to find something new because if I have to go into that office with that depressing lighting and those ugly cubicles one more time, I'm not sure what I'm going to do, as I just can't take it any more since that meeting last month with the boss went so poorly and ..."

Right

- "For family reasons, we're moving to Santa Monica to be closer to my wife's parents. I've had a successful career in CPG marketing and I'm looking for a VP marketing position at a similar company where I can apply my expertise in direct marketing, brand development and public relations."

- "I've really enjoyed leading the development of software at B2B companies, and I'd like to find an opportunity at a growing, VC-backed start-up where my skills in building teams, architecting scalable systems and developing code would make a real difference."

- "I've been in pharmaceutical sales management for the past 16 years and have progressed through roles of increasing responsibility. I'm looking to join another pharmaceutical company where I can lead a national sales team and apply my proven track record of beating quota and developing deeper doctor and care-giver relationships."

You know, Mark Twain said, *"I didn't have time to write a short letter, so I wrote a long one instead."*

And making your elevator pitch short but effective is going to take some time. But it's really very important that you're able to briefly and effectively communicate your goals to anybody you'll meet.

That's the only way they'll know what you already know: that you're a valuable professional with a lot to contribute.

Put Aside Your Impatience and Insecurity

BOTH ARE NATURAL; NEITHER IS AN ADVANTAGE. A long, frustrating job hunt can turn around with a single phone call, and there's no advance warning when that call is going to come. Keep plugging so you're always ready.

Beyond our basic rule of thumb—five months plus one for each big change you want to make in your job description—it's hard to calculate a useful average length for a job search. Most use data so broad-based that the number they come up with has little relevance to someone looking for a job in your industry, geographic location, and with your seniority, salary level and individual skill set. A fast-food burger flipper might only take two days to find a new job; it takes a presidential candidate at least two years of solid campaigning to make the cut.

Figure your search will fall somewhere in between.

In the meantime, even on days it's easier just to surf the Web or not do much of anything, do something. Keep moving, and keep your efforts focused. It's almost certain—no matter how good you are at networking or self-promotion or self-presentation or any of the other skills it takes to get a job—you're emphasizing the parts of the process you're good at and shirking the ones you don't like. Do them anyway; check your time log (see Job Search Checklist, page 42) to make sure you're not skimping on those parts or overcompensating by ignoring your strengths.

In the next pages, let's review the job search piece by piece.

Resume Writing and Presentation

CHAPTER 2 OF THIS BOOK will give you in-depth tips on resume writing and presentation. But don't even open to that section until you've gone through a certain amount of objective self-evaluation to identify what you like to do, what you're good at and what an employer would be getting when they get you.

Who are you, really? More, certainly, than appears on your resume. Unfortunately, recruiters, HR professionals and hiring managers don't have time to appreciate the more subtle aspects of your sterling character. The whole application process is designed for the convenience of people on the other side of the application process, giving you limited opportunity to make yourself stand out from the crowd or emphasize the things that would nail down that perfect job offer if they were obvious.

How do you do that? Show your value.

Would you buy a car or computer without a clear idea of what it would do for you, or even something more subtle, like what using it said about you to other people? Think hard about who you are, what you like to do, and what is the most positive, powerful thing you offer. Then boil that down into a three- to five-word tagline.

Are you an IT professional? So are a lot of other people. An IT professional who's worked closely with business leaders to cut operating costs and increase efficiency? Try, "I'm a technology leader who streamlines operations to maximize profits." Whatever it is, it has to be short, memorable and demonstrate the unique value you bring to the equation.

Create Your Brand

BRAND IS MORE THAN A NAME and a logo. It includes the design of a product and the experience the consumer has using it, as well as all the marketing and advertising activity that surrounds it. Right at the beginning of your search, decide what job you are looking for and what, specifically, you're offering, including your unique value and approach. Then make sure your resume, references, background, job-searching techniques, and even your clothes, grooming and behavior reflect that.

Cut Your Cover Letter

YOUR COVER LETTER SHOULD BE ONLY two or three paragraphs at most. It should make one or two points about why you are perfect for the job and the company, why you're different from all the other candidates applying to the same position, or what you've accomplished in similar positions in the past. It should explain any quirks or open questions, such as a reason you're particularly interested in working for that company, whether you plan to move to the area where the job is located, or why you're applying to an industry or job type that's different from others on your resume.

You should also tell the company when you plan to contact them and thank them for the time they took reading your letter. If you kept things short and efficient enough, they'll be ready to give you a call, not take a nap after slogging through your application opus.

Write Your Resume

THERE ARE MANY RULES TO WRITE A RESUME, but they all boil down to two things: It has to be easy to read, and the message it conveys needs to be clear. It doesn't have to include every job you've ever had or every accomplishment that made you proud. It should contain your unique value proposition, a summary of your skills and experience, a reference to your key stories, and a job progression that led up to your previous job and on to the position you're seeking.

All the information should support the goal you list, and the goal you list should match with the company or industry you're sending the resume to. You should have a generic

TEN Qs TO ASK YOURSELF

1. Which job titles or categories that fit your background have the best prospects? What are the leading companies in that area and how can you best contact them?

2. What's the state of your finances? How much time do you have before you risk losing the house or other financial disaster?

3. Are you willing to relocate for work?

4. Are you willing to change industries?

5. Are you willing to take a step back in either compensation or responsibility? (Do you really need to, or is that fear talking?)

6. How much can you network? Who do you know and how can you contact them to see what they know about the job situation?

7. What professional organizations exist in your industry that you can either join or work more energetically for contacts and job prospects?

8. Who do you know who's been hiring lately or has been hired? Is his experience relevant to you?

9. How many contacts—new contacts, job ads responded to, cold calls made, networking meetings taken—do you aim to make every week?

10. What tools will you use to set goals and keep yourself motivated and on track?

resume that can be applied to a number of potential jobs, but you should also be able to tailor your resume to demonstrate how your experience clearly relates to the functions or responsibilities the company is looking for.

You can also go one step further in your analysis of a job ad or notice. Don't just look at the requirements that are listed. Look at what those requirements indicate about the problems the company is trying to solve. Then use your cover letter and resume to address those problems, not just the language used in the ad.

Resume formats are a lot more flexible than many people believe, though not as much as they'd want. Most list jobs and skills and don't highlight the unique value a person brought to an individual position. Rather than say "was responsible for budget of ... ," try, "cut operational costs by ..." or "increased revenue by focusing on ..." Identifying how your work furthered the ultimate goal of the company is a lot more telling than listing your job functions.

Accomplishments outside work can also play a role. Laura Warren, who used TheLadders to help her in a recent job search, ran her own global cosmetics company for nine years after a long career in shipping and logistics. Even after leaving the shipping world, she continued working in groups that represented the business community of Los Angeles and important non-governmental groups, often fighting for or against legislation she believed would affect the economy of southern California. Integrating all her top-level "extracurricular" work helped recharge her professional focus.

A resume writer at TheLadders helped Jill G., a marketing manager for biotech and veterinary medical manufacturers, focus her efforts and sell herself after she and her husband moved to Texas to get away from cold Iowa winters.

"It was all about specific ways you helped a company move forward," Jill says. "In the interview, too, you have to walk in and tell them exactly what you can do for them and tell about a time in the past that you did that for someone else. I told [a prospective employer] that I had once worked for a company that, among other things, made toothpaste and toothbrushes for dogs and cats. I said, 'If I can sell a toothbrush for a cat, I can sell anything.'"

DIGITAL JOB SEARCH GOTTA DOS

- **Tune your resume.** Make it the best, most concise, most focused, most searchable document you can.

- **Get your resume online and searchable;** it can take over the search for jobs while you're doing other things.

- **Apply only to jobs that are right for you.** Don't waste time tuning letters and resumes for jobs you don't want, even if they're the only ones you can think to apply to right now.

- **Save your searches.** Don't retype the same queries several times a day.

- **Sign up for e-mail alerts.** Sites such as TheLadders let you create search agents and e-mail you when a job opens up—often at the companies in which you're most interested.

- **Work with recruiters.** Find the ones who work in your area and put yourself on their agendas.

- **Don't ever be offline.** Even when you are offline, don't ever stop searching or thinking about your search. That way you're always ready to jump on an opportunity or a tip when it arises.

- **Create a "plan of attack."** Random job searching doesn't work any better than random weight-loss or investment strategies. Evaluate the health of particular industries by evaluating the number of jobs available that are relevant to your skills.

Networking: Keep Your Friends Close and Competitors Closer

CALLING A FRIEND OR COLLEAGUE and asking if she knows of a job can be awkward. It's much easier, and more effective, to ask whether that person would be willing to be a reference for you. Friends are happy to help with a reference, and if they know of an opportunity, they can bring that up, too. And don't forget to ask if there's someone they can introduce you to or who you should talk to next. That's how networking works and how you find out about opportunities as soon as they become available.

Networking feels like you're asking one person after another for favors, but it doesn't really work that way. Think of any professional gathering at which you've met someone who shook your hand and spent the whole conversation looking over your shoulder for someone better to talk to. Now think about the person who asked questions about you and your situation and offered intelligent comments, even if he or she didn't have anything specific to offer. Who would you rather help when you got a call later on?

Recently, Esther G. was laid off from her job as lawyer for a major financial-services company. When talking either to hiring managers or networking contacts, she asks what she can do to help them. "Sometimes they mention something, but mostly I think ahead of time what I can offer—services, references, whatever. If someone's going on a trip to India, I give them tips on where to eat, what to do. It takes a lot of research, but whatever I have, I give. So far, I've gotten three other people jobs. That extends my network even further, and those people will remember me."

Want to multiply your job-searching abilities 500 percent?

Jim Villwock, founder of Job Doctors International LLC, suggests forming a job-search support group with five other people looking for jobs similar to yours. Meet once a week or every other week to share tips on who's hiring, what openings might be coming up, what companies are laying off or hiring—all your actionable intelligence, and theirs.

Sounds like inviting your competition to eat your lunch but, according to Villwock and several executives he's coached, it actually extends your reach far more than it limits your chances. No two people have identical skills and background, and no two hiring managers are looking for exactly the same things. So even if you end up losing an opportunity to someone from your group, odds are that person would have been hired anyway because his or her qualifications and personality are a better fit with the hiring manager. In the meantime, you will have been benefiting from a potential competitor's knowledge, advice and support. And he or she will remember you afterward, becoming a valuable source for opportunities now and in the future.

In this spirit, don't count anyone out of your network. We like the advice of Lynne Waymon, co-founder of career- and networking-coaching consultancy Contacts Count. "You've got four networks," she says. "Take a pencil and divide a sheet of paper in four (see Networking Cheat Sheet, page 51). In one corner you have your Worknet; these are the people you work with. Since you got laid off, they may have been too, or might be, so these are really tenuous right now.

"To the right is your Orgnet; that's for people who work for the same company but not in the same department. Clever networkers build that Orgnet so they know people in other teams and geographical areas that can be useful; you might end up working as the only one with your skills in a different department, for example.

"In the upper left corner is your Pronet—people you know professionally who do the same kind of work, but not at your company. Those are very valuable for specific leads, even in a bad market," Waymon explains. "In the last corner is your Lifenet—your family and friends. Most people quarantine their Lifenet, but that's the place the most unexpected opportunities come from. Your mother-in-law may know someone who should be in your Pronet and who could connect you with someone with a great recommendation for a job. The best networkers are aware of all of these, and the magic is in the synergy."

Interviewing: Make Your Points

IT'S EASY TO FORGET WHEN YOU go into an interview that you're there to press your agenda as well as satisfy the hiring company's. Think ahead of time about the points you want to make and write them down. You could have 10 important things to say, but that number is hard for you to get through and hard for an interviewer to remember.

Think three. Write up three key talking points that are relevant to the company and the job involved and make sure you address each one during the interview. And don't be afraid to refer to your notes during the interview; it shows you've prepared ahead of time, not that you can't remember what you wanted to say. HR professionals or hiring managers will appreciate your level of preparation.

Demonstrate your effectiveness by planning what to elaborate on. There's a story behind every item on your

INTERVIEW DOS AND DON'TS

DO:

- Pick your two or three most memorable or clear successes and practice telling a short (very short!) story about each

- Keep your descriptions high-level enough to be easily understood but detailed enough for the listener to know what you were facing. ("In the XX industry, YY costs are always a concern, and ours were rising. After investigating, I discovered that ZZ was making the problem worse, so what I did was ... ")

DON'T:

- Get into any of the personalities of people you used to work with

- Assume the interviewer knows a lot about the company or industry you were working in

- Overexplain the context of any particular success or challenge

resume—sometimes one with real drama. You can't tell every story about your past to a new employer, or you turn into white noise. The incidents might appear as a quick mention in the resume or cover letter ("saved $100,000 in monthly operational costs ..."). The whole story should only come out in conversation, as a way to demonstrate your bona fides.

Is It Your Age or Your Salary?

LOTS OF MID-CAREER EXECUTIVES BELIEVE they've been passed over at some point because of their age. Age may be an issue, but more often it's the knee-jerk reaction of a youngish HR screener or the size of a candidate's required compensation that's the issue. It's perfectly fair to use a resume that only lists dates for the past 10 or 12 years rather than for every job you've ever had. Gray hair could surprise an interviewer who'd missed the possibility that a candidate is middle-aged, but there are ways to deal with that once you're in the door.

First, focus on demonstrating that health, energy or salary level are not issues for you. This will take a bit of preparation, as you want to get this information across on your own terms. The point is to convince an HR screener that you can take the next step and be passed along in the interview process. The key to overcoming age or any other potential obstacle during the interview isn't to pretend it doesn't exist or hope it doesn't come up. It's to speak directly to it before the subject even gets raised, often during the first few minutes of an interview, which is more small talk than real discussion.

"If age might be an issue and someone asks, 'How are you?' or 'How was your weekend?' instead of the usual you can go out of your way to say, 'I went hiking with some buddies of mine over the weekend and I feel great!' " suggests Cheryl Palmer, president of CalltoCareer.com. "Right at the outset you paint this picture of someone who's energetic and raring to go. You've painted over those misgivings without even knowing if age would be an issue."

If a hiring manager asks you about salary, focus on the value you provide: "The value I'll bring to your organization will beat any salary I require. Let's talk about that value, then work on a way you can bring me on board in a way that's comfortable for you."

No matter how stressed you are, be polite to everyone you meet at the company where you're interviewing. You never know who the hiring manager will talk to. Don't trash-talk your previous bosses or others in the industry; it only gives the interviewer a negative impression of you. Don't talk money until the end of the discussion; focus on the job and your capabilities. Thank the interviewer for his time and attention, then send a thank-you e-mail saying it again and reiterating the

HOW TO WORK WITH EXECUTIVE RECRUITERS

You met with a recruiter, but now she's not responding to your e-mails. Maybe your background is perfect but you don't make it past the phone screen. How could it be that you're "not a good fit" when you're so clearly made for the position? Below are some typical scenarios in which job seekers may find themselves.

SCENARIO ONE

You think you're a perfect fit for the position, yet the recruiter isn't responding to your application or your follow-up calls and e-mails.

The Verdict: You're not qualified for the job.
The Logic: Like it or not, your work experience may not fit the bill.

It could be that the hiring company is looking for 10 years of sales experience and that your 15 is not attractive. It's also possible that you didn't read the posting closely, or at all. "When a job seeker ignores certain stipulations, such as a listing that requests local candidates only or has degree requirements that don't match, it becomes evident that they are answering postings without reading them," says one recruiter at a search firm in Chicago. "This is a waste of time for everyone involved as well as frustrating for a recruiter."
The Fix: Time to move on.

The Verdict: You're a good fit but not an ideal fit.

The Logic: Third-party recruiting agencies get paid a lot of money to find people that a corporation in need of staff can't. With a 15 percent to 25 percent fee going to the recruiter, corporations want to make sure they hire the right person. In plenty of cases, *almost* isn't good enough.
The Fix: Try focusing on your "transferable skills"—the core abilities that make you valuable across industries and functions. Perhaps these skills can close the qualification gap.

The Verdict: Your recruiter—or the hiring company—isn't effectively communicating the job specifications.
The Logic: Sometimes recruiters aren't able to effectively express what their client is looking for, a result of their own limitations or their client's lack of specificity. The larger the organization, the more red tape there usually is.
The Fix: The recruiter is in a tight spot herself. If you can help suggest the solution that's needed to make the position work, you'll win yourself an important ally.

The Verdict: Your e-mail subject line could be slowing down the process.

The Logic: If a recruiter is sorting through hundreds of e-mails a day, it makes her life easier if she receives a cue about the contents of the e-mail.
The Fix: Effective subject lines in e-mails should reference the position you're applying for, rather than "Hello" or "Intro."

The Verdict: Your resume may not be conveying your story at a glance.
The Logic: If a quick scan does not yield a compelling career narrative, your application may never make it beyond the In box; recruiters often have little time to devote to each resume.
The Fix: Make it easy for recruiters to find what they're looking for: your last employer and position, your tenure there, and the three most relevant bullet points based on the job you're applying for.

The Verdict: Misspellings of any kind turn off recruiters.
The Logic: Typos leave the impression that you don't pay attention to details.
The Fix: Double- and triple-check your cover letter and resume. Better still, have someone with an eye for detail proof it.

The Verdict: A generic cover letter could be your undoing.
The Logic: Recruiters may read the lack of specificity as lazy and/or uncaring.
The Fix: Tailor each letter to the particular company, industry and position to which you're applying.

SCENARIO TWO

You didn't make it past the recruiter's phone screener.

....

The Verdict: Your general attitude could be a mismatch with the hiring company.

The Logic: Your professional-yet-serious demeanor, for example, may not work in a setting where a sense of lightness and humor is considered a priority for managers.

The Fix: Don't take it personally. The longer a recruiter has worked with the hiring company, the better he's able to evaluate your candidacy.

....

The Verdict: You didn't listen to the questions.

The Logic: During phone screens and interviews, less is often more. Whether the cause is nervousness, self-absorption or other limitations, candidates sometimes provide far more information than a question warrants. Marian Rich, a recruiter with Bonell Ryan, a retained search firm in New York, says she often asks candidates to give a quick overview of their careers, probing for details later in the process. "I'm always dismayed at how many candidates launch into an in-depth and very lengthy response," Rich observes. "It can put me off and will certainly raise the question of whether or not this candidate will interview well with a client."

The Fix: Follow up with the recruiter to ask her why you're not a good fit. She should be able to

provide a concrete reason. If she can do that—and you trust her assessment—let her know you'd like to be considered for future positions.

SCENARIO THREE

You met the recruiter in person, but now he doesn't think you're right for the job.

....

The Verdict: Your work style may not be suited to the position.

The Logic: The recruiter may determine that you thrive in structured work settings, for example, but the hiring company is looking for someone who functions best in an unstructured environment.

The Fix: Once again, recruiters who have placed candidates with the hiring company have a good sense of who would succeed there. It is well within your rights to ask how long the recruiter has worked with a certain company.

....

The Verdict: Your personality may not be a match for certain company or department cultures.

The Logic: For instance, you may think your ambition and assertive personality could only be an asset, but it could signal potential challenges at some firms. "If a candidate has career aspirations and I pick up that they may not have patience before they see advancement or will be badgering HR in regards to advancement, they may not be right for

certain companies," says Harold Laslo, with The Aldan Troy Group, a recruiting firm in New York, adding that small companies tend to be more focused on personality than large ones.

The Fix: Talk to your recruiter and find out exactly why you're no longer in the running. Gather as much information as you can and ask if there's anything about your personal performance that you could improve.

SCENARIO FOUR

The recruiter is being vague about why the hiring company doesn't want to proceed with your application.

....

The Verdict: She may not have all the information.

The Logic: At each point in the application process, your recruiter should be able to cite specific reasons why she (or the hiring company) doesn't think you're a suitable candidate for the job. But recruiters don't always have that information if the hiring company is reticent to disclose it for legal or other reasons.

The Fix: Don't take it out on the recruiter. It's easy to become frustrated and conclude this individual is giving you the runaround; understanding the role each of you plays in the job search will be more productive than treating the recruiter as an adversary.

Your Role—and the Recruiter's

RECRUITERS AND JOB SEEKERS each have roles to play every step of the way. Make sure you do your part.

> **Recruiter works closely with the hiring company to shape a specific and accurate job description**

> **Job seeker submits resume**

Job seeker's role: Follow directions, tailor your cover letter and make sure it is typo-free. If you're sending your resume by e-mail, use a subject line that includes the position for which you're applying. Don't apply for a job for which you know you're not qualified. Call to make sure the recruiter received your resume, but don't try to sell yourself during that conversation.

Recruiter's role: She may call or send an automated reply, but courtesy calls are rare in recruiting. If she thinks you're potentially a good fit, she'll be in touch. If not, she won't have the time because she's sorting through hundreds of other applications.

> **Recruiter evaluates application and possibly discusses job seeker's resume with hiring company**

> **Phone interview**

Job seeker's role: Learn as much as you can about the job. Present yourself in the best possible light. Be forthcoming. Answer questions directly and avoid longwinded explanations. Make sure the recruiter leaves the conversation with a meaningful sense of what you would bring to the position.

Recruiter's role: Clarify work history. Evaluate general attitude and screen for cultural fit. Possibly confirm compensation requirements.

> **In-person meeting with recruiter**

Job seeker's role: Prove that you're a polished professional with the talent and skill set required. Answer questions with care, keeping in mind that the recruiter can help you get to the next step. If you're dismissive or cavalier, the recruiter may not want to risk introducing you to the hiring company.

Recruiter's role: Learn more about what's not in a resume or cover letter, e.g., personality quirks and work style. Determine that everything in the resume is legitimate and factual. Communicate to candidate how he could improve interview performance.

Prep for interview with hiring company

Job seeker's role: Gather as much information as possible about what the hiring manager is looking for, who you'll be meeting with and potential questions he might ask.

Recruiter's role: Help candidate understand what she can expect from the interview, including who she will be meeting with and what she should emphasize with certain interviewers. Good recruiters will relay obstacles that past candidates encountered when interviewing at the hiring company.

Interview with client

Hiring company discusses job seekers with recruiter

Recruiter and job seeker talk post-interview

Job seeker's role: Do not disappear. If you don't get in touch quickly, it may give the impression of disinterest, regardless of the circumstances. At every touch point, you should remind the recruiter how reliable you are. If you're absolutely not interested in the position and wouldn't consider accepting an offer, don't say that you are.

No offer

Job seeker's role: Accept feedback graciously. Don't be irrational or belligerent. Find out more about why you weren't a match. If the recruiter isn't being specific, ask for more information. If could be that the company is being reticent.

Recruiter's role: Provide specific reasons why the company didn't think the job seeker was a good fit.

Offer

Job seeker's role: Gather information about compensation, bonus structure and benefits. Respond as quickly as possible without rushing the decision.

Recruiter's role: Communicate terms of offer. Some hiring companies prefer to discuss components of the package directly with the job seeker. Gauge job seeker's level of interest.

points you wanted to make about yourself. It acknowledges the interviewer's time and gives you one more opportunity to make a targeted impression.

Closing the Deal:
Negotiating Compensation

WHEN YOU'RE INTERVIEWING, be prepared to answer questions about your compensation requirements. It's a touchy subject, but you can get a good idea of market values through your personal networking or by researching salaries online at Glassdoor.com, Salary.com, Payscale.com and other sites. Even more accurate is information from professional organizations such as Financial Executives International, which polls members about compensation and working conditions.

If the job is more junior than you're looking for or the salary is too low, don't be afraid to offer alternatives. You can take the job at the top available salary, even if it's below what you need, but ask for a salary review after six months and define the value you can deliver that would merit an increase. You can also take the job on a consulting basis with the potential to shift to full time later on. "Make the entry point as comfortable as possible for them," counsels Sally Haver, senior vice president of business development at The Ayers Group/Career Partners International, a recruiting company that specializes in career transitions and outplacement.

Just like selling a product, the key in landing a good job with the right salary is demonstrating value. Most executives can say they have 20 years experience, "but often it's one year of experience 20 times," explains Villwock. The key is to show not just that you can elegantly do the kinds of things a less experienced person can't do at all but to show how your experience and value has grown and what, specifically, that experience can help you do for the company you're talking to.

That requires research, though: talking to people inside the industry and the company and reading everything you can about it to know what problems it's facing and how it prefers to operate. Don't focus on how you manage people or issues within your own department; focus on how a department you lead will save money or generate revenue. "If I'm the CEO or CFO or COO, I care about return on investment, cost savings, how you're going to help me increase revenue, not how you're going to train people in your department," Villwock says. "That said, to me you're not a commodity and, to me as the CEO, that you can do things to solve the problems I'm worried about."

Change Your Industry, Change Your Luck

WHEN AN INDUSTRY FACES ECONOMIC ADVERSITY, top recruiters see a flood of applications from people eager to get out of a tight market and apply their skills in another. It's a good tactic, and one that can enrich and extend your career, according to some veteran industry switchers. Switching industries tends to be easier for more junior people and smoother for those who have moved from one industry to another throughout their careers than for those who have worked in only one market.

But it is doable, even for senior executives with a long history in one industry and even in a market in which employers are demanding very specific sets of skills, according to Robert Hawthorne, president of Hawthorne Executive Search, a member of TheLadders' community of recruiters.

About a quarter to a third of the placements in which Hawthorne is involved will entail a client hiring someone for an executive slot who has little or no experience in that particular industry. "I call it the best-athlete scenario," he says. "If you get a real star, someone with a legacy of accomplishment, who has a passion for what they do, I'll tell a company they should interview this person anyway."

"We have seen a lot of career changing over the past couple of years," observes Michael Neece, chief strategy officer of PongoResume, an automated resume-writing service, and InterviewMastery.com, a job-interview training site. "Upwards of 27 percent of our clients are either changing industries or coming back into the workforce after time away."

The recommendations of trusted recruiters (who may have worked with the same set of employers for years and are intimately familiar with the company's needs and culture) are incredibly important for targeting jobs at the very high end of the job market, according to Sharon D., a former top-level marketing executive with Bear Stearns and other Wall Street companies who left her last job at an investment bank voluntarily.

"[R]ecruiters will have a team for each industry," Sharon says. "The person in financial services can come to a meeting with recruiters specializing in other areas and say, 'I have this great candidate in financial services who wants to make a change,' and pass that person along to the technology group" or other appropriate departments.

But it's not necessary to get heroic assistance from an outside source or from one recruiter who's a particular fan to make the transition successfully, according to Clark Christensen, a career-long industry switcher who is currently chief financial officer of Atlanta-based PS Energy Group Inc.

"All other things being equal, the industry experience does help, but not so much

> Getting out of a tight market and applying your skills in a new field can enrich and extend your career, even for senior executives with a long history in one industry and even in a market in which employers are demanding very specific sets of skills.

that it trumps other factors and other skills," Christensen explains. "You do have to sell to the business you're coming to that you have the skills that are necessary; and once you're in the business, you [have to] understand the industry more and get better at what you do.

"But early on I decided I was the product—that my skill sets and aptitudes and competencies were the product and that they could be applied in more than one industry." Christensen, who started his accounting career as a consultant, moved into international auditing and accounting roles at Coca-Cola, headed up Coke's Moscow bottling operation and advanced to director level before deciding he'd rather live in the United States. Since then, he's been head of financial operations at the retail-services company Miller Zell and chief financial officer of logistics at shipping-service company Global Link Logistics Inc.

Constantly marketing yourself—by taking part in local and national professional groups, networking with both old and new contacts as if you're always looking for a job, and keeping your resume fresh and available—is critical to broadening your career options and finding openings in industries outside your own experience, Christensen has found.

Unless you're in one of the core functions of an industry—an investment analyst at a brokerage, for example, or an underwriter in insurance—it's not that hard to separate your job functions from the industry in which you work, according to Neece.

"Industry experience is highly overvalued," Neece says. "Someone could work in a core operation, but her personal core skill set is being a salesperson; when she's looking to make transitions from one industry to another, she's just looking for a way to do a similar thing in a different place."

It's also possible, Neece points out, to freshen your career prospects by changing departments rather than changing employers or industries. "When I was at Fidelity, we had equity and fixed-income analysts who were tired of doing the same thing every day. One of the things people did was go into compliance, where they were charged with making sure the composition of portfolios they'd been building was in compliance with company policies. Or you could move from the trading floor to being a recruiter looking for other people with similar skills. Take baby steps instead of a big shift."

How to Package and Manage Yourself

THE KEY TO MAKING THE MOVE SUCCESSFUL is not only to inventory your own skills but to package them so they're appropriate for the industry you're targeting, according to Palmer.

The only way to do that is to understand the specific requirements of the

FIVE WAYS TO MAKE YOUR RECRUITER'S JOB EASIER

1. Don't try to be a square peg in a round hole. If the company is looking for a candidate with 10 years of experience in small companies, don't act as if your 20 years at large companies isn't right there on paper. "Nothing would make us happier than saying, 'Yes, this is a good fit,' " says Marian Rich of Bonell Ryan. "But our clients pay us to bring candidates who most closely align with their ideal profile."

2. Don't be cagey about compensation. The first question that hiring managers tend to ask recruiters is how much the job seeker is earning. So when candidates hesitate to disclose their compensation or instead inquire about what the pro- spective job would pay, Rich takes pause, wondering why the candidate is not forthcoming. "It is always better to be as honest as possible around issues concerning compensation," Rich explains.

3. Establish an understanding about phone calls and e-mails. If your every phone call is not promptly returned, it could be that the recruiter is extremely busy or that your background won't help him fill an immediate position. While you may disagree, sending frequent or belligerent e-mails won't change his mind and may make him not want to work with you on future positions.

4. After your interview with the hiring company, contact your recruiter right away. You may feel like the interview was lousy, but it's your responsibility to let the recruiter know how it went. "The lack of follow-up may show a level of disinterest, which isn't always the case," notes Harold Laslo of the Aldan Troy Group.

5. Refer talented friends and colleagues to your recruiter. It could only work to your advantage to recommend talented people to your recruiter(s), even for a role that you wanted. Your recruiter will appreciate the help and he may return the favor in the future.

industry and change the way you'd do your job. Understanding an industry at that level isn't difficult but does require research, Palmer advises, whether that means reading reports on hiring or outsourcing trends in the industry from the Bureau of Labor Statistics or taking a contact from that industry out to lunch to pick his or her brain about the job market.

"Employers don't want a long learning curve," Palmer insists. "They want someone who can speak the lingo and hit the ground running. The trick is to convince them that you can contribute right away. So read trade journals, talk to insiders, and get a really good handle on what's going on in that industry and in that company in particular."

Another alternative is to become a pioneer within the same company rather than leaving to do innovative things, according to Josh Klenoff, president of JK-Coaching.com.

"I had one client who didn't like the company he worked in but ended up pitching a new type of business to management and leading that himself. He was happier there than he would have been leaving for another job," Klenoff says. "One mistake people make early in their careers is that they cede management of themselves to their managers. But no manager will ever care as much about your career as you do yourself."

It's important to make a regular assessment of your job skills and think periodically about what direction you want your career to take. But it's critical to be able to do that analysis from a potential employer's point of view, not just your own.

"The right skill set is a good starting point," Palmer says, "but you need to present yourself well on paper and articulate what you can do for the employer right off the bat in an interview setting."

Tough Sell: How Specialists Switch Markets

IT'S EMINENTLY POSSIBLE even for a specialist with a long history in one industry to make the switch to another. But there will be some roadblocks to overcome, es-

RESOURCES CHANGING INDUSTRIES

The grass may be greener in another field; these resources can help you over the fence and make your career transition a smooth one.

- From aircraft mechanics to zookeepers, *The Department of Labor's Occupational Outlook Handbook* is a comprehensive resource on almost any job you can think of, including the nature of each position, required training, and estimated salary.

- Professional organizations concentrate vast information about specific career fields, including job opportunities, industry trends and employers in the professions they serve.

- OK, so getting your first AARP card in the mail on your 50th birthday was kind of a shock, and it's odd to

get career advice from a group dedicated to "retired persons." Still, *AARP's National Employer Team* can help, with a network created to make it easier for mature workers to connect to companies that value experience, talent and abilities. Its Web site features information and listings from companies that have made a strong commitment to hiring experienced, executive professionals.

- Career coaches can reality-check your plans, pull out those repressed professional ambitions and encourage you to power over those last few hurdles to your goal. When considering a career coach, check to see that they're accredited with one of the major counseling organizations (such

as the CACREP or NBCC), and that they have experience with career changes.

- It might have been a while since you've heard anything but donation requests from your alma mater. Nevertheless, many schools offer career services for alumni that extend far beyond the first-job search they do for students. In addition to being able to meet with a career counselor, access your alumni network and view job listings provided by your school, you should also enquire about reciprocity programs that could give you access to the career-services offices of colleges and universities in your local area or that are particularly strong in your professional arena. NYU Law is one example.

pecially in sectors of the economy that are especially hard-hit.

"People think, 'I've done sales in my industry; I can do this type of sales,'" according to Hawthorne. "It's not uncommon, but they have to think, 'How can I package myself to compete with someone from this industry?' Frankly, they're not going to stack up well against a performer with experience and a track record in the industry. The out-of-industry candidate is going to be out of luck."

Sharon, the former marketing executive with Bear Stearns, had 24 years in financial services at a very high level. "But recruiters and connections I've spoken with have told me I'm too entrenched," she explains. "All the advice is to take your core competencies and just move them into some other area. A lot of people in those areas just don't want you. They see 'financial services' tattooed on your forehead, and they already have enough people in their own areas."

Making the switch from a Wall Street firm (where both the products and the business are highly complex and don't much resemble the products in other industries) might be harder that switching from a less-arcane industry, according to Christensen.

"Industries like that make you highly specialized, and you get paid highly for it," Christensen says. "But you've taken a little bit of a fork in the road, and you've got to come back a bit if you're going to change directions."

The more industry-specific your knowledge or experience, however, the more difficult it is to apply it elsewhere.

"I'm not a chief financial officer," Sharon says. "A chief financial officer or accountant might have an easier time. I'd be aiming for direct sales. But really, is a fantastic product marketer or strategist who has built sales strategies for every type of financial product around not going to be able to market other things?"

To a certain extent, complexity is complexity, so the ability to handle the technicalities of one industry is a good indication you could do the same in another. Neece, who worked in human resources at Hewlett-Packard, Fidelity and publishing giant International Data Group, says the key to convincing an interviewer of your competency is to show how you mastered the complexities of your last industry and do enough research to show you understand a fair amount of the subtleties of the new one as well.

"If you've made the decision to switch and are having a hard time selling it, go back to the common threads that transfer across industries," Christensen says. He suggests you tell interviewers, "'I was in this industry, and this is what I did, but there were 10 or 12 subindustries in there. I learned each one quickly to get the job done, and isn't that what you're looking for?'

"You have to get the interview, let them see the passion in your eye and show them you're not stuck and that you have these skills that make you more than your resume would suggest," Christensen believes.

Your Job Application's Journey

JOB SEEKERS OFTEN COMPLAIN that potential employers more closely resemble black holes than functioning companies. Submitted resumes—even those addressed to specific managers and hand-carried by contacts on the inside—often get no response. Even after several stages of screening and in-person interviews, thank-you notes and inquiries, job seekers often find themselves in a dead zone where all communication ceases, despite their best efforts and best-laid plans.

What happened?

"The black hole is alive and well, and that's really a shame," says David A. Earle, managing partner at Staffing.org, an analyst company that measures recruiting trends. "We've taken a fairly strident position that corporations that don't change

HIRED!
FROM FAMILY PLUMBING BUSINESS TO SALES

Mid-career job seekers trying to break into a new industry often complain that it feels as if they're fighting the momentum of their previous work history. Dan Rozelman was contending with three generations of family history when he switched industries, first shutting down his plumbing business to sell manufacturing equipment, then to manage a staff selling glass to window manufacturers.

"Sales was always my forte," he said. Through TheLadders, Rozelman found and accepted a sales-management job that moves him toward the career goal he set for himself, though in a different part of the business from the one in which he started.

Rozelman started his post-college career with a two-year stint selling truck parts across

most of the Midwest before coming home to start his own plumbing business in 1998. He specialized in new construction—installing the plumbing for all the houses in a new development or new commercial or residential buildings.

IDENTIFYING KEY STRENGTHS
"I was doing a million a year in new construction running two crews," Rozelman says. "I could have run 15 crews, but I couldn't find the right people to oversee the work to the level it needed to be done."

The inability to scale finally frustrated Rozelman enough that he decided to get out of the plumbing business and focus on sales instead. Taking an inventory of his own skills, Rozelman

decided his nine years in the construction business had given him enough understanding and insight that he could operate in any business closely related to it.

"My strengths were in talking to contractors, owners of contracting companies, supply houses," Rozelman says. "I knew the lingo; understood what was going on. I knew what the end users of the product had to deal with on a daily basis."

It took six months of research and applying to online job ads. "I got a lot of interviews, and tried to make most of what I said specific to the type of sale and challenge I was applying for. I talked about how I would spec a job with the engineers and sell the job and present it. I could say, 'I know you're selling to the end user, and in my position,

their way of doing things in this Internet-centric environment will start to encounter candidates that know they're being treated well at Place A and badly at Place B, and that knowledge will start showing up in those companies' recruiting."

But a better understanding of the application process can help illuminate the black hole and help job seekers prepare for the lack of response and abrupt replies they're likely to encounter during the job search.

Why aren't recruiters more responsive? The No. 1 reason is the sheer volume of candidates. "We're getting so many resumes these days and so many people will apply for a job that they're not qualified for that it's a big stretch for HR people or recruiters to get back in touch with every single person," says Lindsay Olson, a partner and recruiter at Paradigm Staffing, a recruiting company that specializes in marketing and PR positions.

Unexpected kinks in the process notwithstanding, every application goes

I did this. This is what drives their decisions, and this is what their purchasing patterns are and how they work with engineers and this is what they're concerned about.'"

RE-REINVENTING

There was a certain amount of luck in landing the job, he admits. But in 18 months he outstripped the expectations the company had set for him.

His territory covered 19 states, and the average sale was close to half a million dollars. Long-term capital equipment isn't a high-turnover business, though, so the customer he sold a welding or fitting machine to one year might not buy again for six years.

It took about another six months, this time using TheLadders as his primary source of job postings, newsletters and advice on resume format, to find his current job as sales manager for a Cleveland-based company that manufactures double-paned insulated glass.

"I wasn't looking for something too specific—an industry or business that was growing and had some opportunity to move up," he said.

When he got an interview, he relied on his knowledge of the construction business, sales and negotiation. When they asked, "What do you know about glass?" Rozelman said, "If I can learn all the ins and outs of the capital equipment to make vinyl windows and break into some of the customers and get the letters of thanks on those com-plicated sales—no offense, but glass has got to be a breeze!'"

LOOKING FORWARD

Rozelman supervises three other salespeople covering a territory about 300 miles in every direction from Cleveland. The money is better, the work is interesting and there's a growth path.

"The president and vice president are only going to be in the company another five years or so, and my boss, the vice president of sales, can probably step up to the vice president's job, and I can move into his," Rozelman says.

"Plus, they're looking to do a major expansion into the East Coast, and I'd be responsible for helping to grow business. It's a good opportunity."

through certain steps and an expected timeline. That doesn't mean the process won't get short-circuited, sidetracked or altered along the way, but understanding the typical flow of a job application can help an expectant applicant adjust his expectations.

1. Resume goes in ...

Whether you're responding to an ad on TheLadders, a special-purpose job site, or working with a contact at the company who can hand-deliver your resume to the hiring manager, your resume and cover letter are going to be screened by someone. More often than not, it's a third-party recruiter who gets paid only when a hire is made, and might not get hired again for presenting any but the most appropriate candidates—and not too many of them.

"We might present three to the client, and we decide on those by sifting through resumes, doing initial interviews and asking extra questions about topics the client might want more information about than the resume says," according to Olson. "We try to get some kind of response out within 48 hours, at least acknowledging that we got your resume. Most companies don't even do that."

Next, most large companies feed the resumes into an Applicant Tracking System (ATS) database, then use search keywords to match candidates to the job description and build a list of suitable candidates to interview. At this point, someone inside the company is finally looking at your resume; to get any further, your credentials must make a good impression the moment an HR screener or hiring manager sees them.

"People have no attention spans; they have no time to read, so if you think you're a good fit, list all their requirements down the left side of the paper and all the experiences you have that answer each one on the right side," suggests Haver. "Show them how you match up on each point, and make it really short—less than one page."

2. You've been picked

If you are one of the lucky ones to get a screening call, expect it to last about half an hour, be reasonably pleasant and leave you with very little idea whether you will progress to the next stage.

Recruiters are looking for how well a candidate communicates, how she comes across on the phone, and whether she'll be a good match in personality and work expectations for the hiring manager. It's a judgment call for the recruiter.

"Even if you look like a very good candidate, that person is probably in the middle of screening a lot of candidates, so you might be the leading candidate when you hang up but not later on," Olson says. "You should ask at the end of that conversation, 'What's the next step?' and they might tell you they'll send your name on to the client. But recruiters could have a lot of reasons for saying it but not doing it."

Among those reasons: Better candidates might crop up, the recruiter might be trying to avoid giving a candidate bad news or the hiring company might change the criteria for the job.

Ask at the end of the interview whether you'll be passed on to the next step, but don't expect always to know whether it will actually happen. Your best bet is to call the recruiter back a few days or a week later to touch base.

3. Presentation behind closed doors

The next stage is completely out of your control, so you should try not to worry about it. Once the screening interviews are finished, the recruiter or internal HR manager will present the top candidates to the hiring manager or managers. Usually that will happen within a day or two of completing the screening calls. Many companies require more than one decision-maker to sign off on hires or even which candidates to interview.

Recruiters present a candidate's strengths to show where he matches the description laid out by the hiring manager, and describe weak points such as the lack of proficiency in the particular software package the hiring company uses.

"With the number of candidates they have, hiring managers are incredibly picky," Haver says. "If they lay out 10 requirements, they want 10 for 10, not nine out of 10."

In most cases, it takes less than a week to get that sign-off and an indeterminate time to set up and conduct in-person interviews. If you haven't heard from the recruiter or the company within a week or two, don't count on hearing back.

4. Audition and follow-up

From the hiring manager's perspective, the interview and immediate aftermath can be like judging a children's talent contest in a town where you know all the parents, according to Haver.

"People inside are leaning on the hiring managers," she says.

"It's unbelievable how much pressure some of them are getting from people who want to find a spot for their brother-in-law or friend who can't pay the mortgage and needs a job, or someone inside. Everyone's flagging their own candidate, so if you're outside and don't have a champion, it's hard to stay at the top of the list."

Still, as with the screening interview, cover your bases. Keep in touch with the hiring manager, if possible. If not, contact the HR manager or third-party recruiter. Send a thank-you note. Phone the recruiter a few days later to see how it goes, and about once a week thereafter. Any less and you will lose touch; any more and you will overstay your welcome.

"It's perfectly fair to expect to know what's going on and what you can expect, but it doesn't always happen," says Olson. If you get no response at all, either to the interview or the thank-you and follow-up notes, that's a bad sign. It's possible hiring managers are having trouble coordinating, but more likely they've made a decision that doesn't include you and don't want to call to confirm it.

One word of advice from Olson: Don't go around the recruiter and call the hiring manager directly. "That's a good way to get them annoyed and wanting to not work with you again," Olson cautions.

And don't call more than once a week or so to check, even if the ad is still up weeks or months after your interview. Ads might be posted automatically to hundreds of job boards or might go up as part of a longer-term contract with mass-market job sites. Often the ads remain online long after the job was filled because the company's ad buy required that it be listed for 30, 60 or 90 days—far longer than it might be valid.

"I've seen companies take six months to make a decision, though," Olson says. "Not hearing doesn't necessarily mean it's gone. If they're open with you and tell you why there's a delay, go ahead and stick with it. But don't stop looking for other things."

What if Companies Treated Job Applicants Like Customers?

The resume black hole is alive and well. Know how the process works and you might be able to avoid the darkness— or at least adjust your expectations.

WHEN A CUSTOMER PICKS UP the phone to call the help desk at Hewlett-Packard, several things happen that let HP deliver the appropriate answer to the caller. Software called a Customer Relationship Management (CRM) system displays the customer's profile to the operator who can see, for instance, that the caller works for a company that just purchased a $1.5 million data-storage solution or that he's just bought a $150 laptop for his son in college. The CRM system lets HP route the call to the right assistance and provide the appropriate level of support. It also lets the company know when the customer might be ready for an upgrade or more products. It is a cornerstone of modern customer service and sales.

The experience for job applicants at most U.S. companies is nearly 180 degrees from this level of customer service. Thanks to the notorious resume "black hole," they submit their resumes and never hear back from the company. They call and write e-mails repeatedly but get no response. They may even progress through the process to several rounds of interviews, only to be left in the dark when the company decides not to hire them.

So why is it that customers are treated so well and applicants, so poorly?

The technology is there, but the incentive is not. Few companies see happy applicants as a business imperative and can't justify the expense of adding CRM capabilities to the process. Recruiters and hiring managers are halfway there, says Earle. Most companies already use ATS software to manage and track job candidates. CRM capabilities would extend the ATS to set engagement standards, such as deadlines to respond to applicants, alerts when a job has been filled or the applicant is disqualified so a recruiter can send a response, and automatic suggestions for future job openings.

"Merging CRM with applicant tracking systems lets you approach staffing in the same way you would a sales territory," Earle explains. "It lets you lay out your brand and presence and become like flypaper for candidates who touch the system—which improves the quality of hiring by more effectively selecting among the available candidates."

So far there are very few companies either willing or interested in the cost and complexity of enhancing their hiring with CRM, Earle admits, although Staffing. org and other research entities promote it as the next major improvement in hiring. It would certainly address the major weakness of electronic hiring processes by giving both recruiters and human-resources professionals the tools to find the right candidates for the right jobs.

HR managers and recruiters don't have the time to invest in follow-up alerts, let alone more high-touch approaches, no matter how effective they might be in the long run, he says. And automation of the process has hurt more than it has helped.

"Computerization was supposed to have solved a lot of problems in the hiring market, but what it did was actually create a whole other set of problems because the number of candidates is vastly greater, but the ability to parse that information effectively is not," Earle says. "Tens of millions of applications create a sea of information, but the picture doesn't become clearer when you need it to; it remains just a sea of information, which leaves companies just as frustrated as candidates."

The current buyer's market exacerbates the problem. Because companies have plenty of candidates to choose from, they feel no need to please the applicant.

Companies such as J.P. Morgan, IBM and Deloitte have all created social networks that resemble LinkedIn or Facebook, says Kate Lukach, director of marketing for software provider SelectMinds, but these networks are limited to current employees and alumni and are designed to help drive new business and new hires from former employees back to the company.

Being able to filter a sea of applicants to a pool of qualified candidates not only makes HR's job easier and cheaper, it ultimately improves the quality and speed of the hiring process.

CHECKLIST: JOB SEARCH

Keeping ahead of your job search means staying on track. Follow this schedule to keep your career in motion.

DAILY

○ **Create an activity log** and note everything you've done today, this week and this month. Note opportunities, contacts and organizations you need to follow up with and schedule when you should do it.

○ **Check job ads** on TheLadders.com; local job-ad sites; and the job boards of any professional organizations, alumni organizations, social networks or other clubs, referral networks or affinity groups to which you belong.

○ **Make and return calls.**

○ **Make at least one call to a new networking contact;** return a call to a net-working colleague who has called you.

○ **Phone a former colleague** to get an update on the market, gossip about the old crowd or just shoot the breeze. Talking to people who are still in the business keeps you mentally connected to the environment and reminds former colleagues that you and your skills are still available.

WEEKLY

○ **Follow up on resumes** you've sent or screening calls you've gotten. Don't stalk recruiters or hiring managers, but do make sure you're up-to-date on all your main prospects.

○ **Make a list of all your potential networking contacts** and areas you might not have explored yet.

MONTHLY

○ **Sharpen your job-hunting strategy;** identify areas that are most and least productive and those you haven't exploited far enough.

○ **Evaluate your collateral material**—talking points for the interview, tag line for the resume and introductions, elevator pitch for the resume and opening conversations.

GETTING ORGANIZED

Name three other professionals you'd like to meet to learn about their companies or functions:

1. _____

2. _____

3. _____

○ **Activity tracking:** Do you have a system for documenting networking occasions, applications, material exchanged with potential employers and any other event (big or small) that puts you in contact with someone who can help you get your next job?

○ **Schedules:** Do you have a consistent, well-documented weekly routine that includes job-seeking activities as well as personal time? Can you look up what you did for your job search the Thursday before last?

TARGET COMPANY LIST

Company Name	Company URL	HQ Location	Industry

Found employees/ former employees in network?	If so, contacted network?	Applied to jobs?

TARGET CONTACT LIST

Name	E-mail	Phone	Company

How you know them?	Contacted? (Date)	Responded? (Date)

JOB APPLICATIONS

Job Title	Company Name	Location	URL
Sample: Director of Sales	Company XZY	New York, NY	www.sampleboard.com/dir_s

Date Resume Submitted	Date Followed Up	Other Comments
April 9, 2010	*April 13, 2010*	*Found job on TheLadders; used cover letter #2 & resume #1 for applicaton*

JOB FIT ANALYSIS

Location	Relevant Skill Set	Industry Experience	Functional Experience	Network	Job Fit
Currently located within commuting distance?	Meets stated job requirements?	Same industry as company's industry?	Same function as role?	Built connections that can help you navigate company?	How many of these attributes fit you?
YES	YES	NO	YES	NO	3/5

NETWORKING CHEAT SHEET

Pronet
People you know professionally who do the same kind of work but not at your company

1. _____
2. _____
3. _____
4. _____
5. _____
6. _____
7. _____
8. _____
9. _____
10. _____

Lifenet
Your family and friends

1. _____
2. _____
3. _____
4. _____
5. _____
6. _____
7. _____
8. _____
9. _____
10. _____

Worknet
People you work with

1. _____
2. _____
3. _____
4. _____
5. _____
6. _____
7. _____
8. _____
9. _____
10. _____

Orgnet
People who work for the same company but not in the same department

1. _____
2. _____
3. _____
4. _____
5. _____
6. _____
7. _____
8. _____
9. _____
10. _____

GAPS IN YOUR RESUME

RESUME OBJECTIVE TO TEL

EIGHT WAYS YOUR RESUME CAN SAY 'I'M UNPROFESSIONAL'

Y

RESU

BRAIN DUMP AND BRAINSTORM

BE CLEAR, AND BE WHAT THEY NEED

L THE TRUTH

OUR

ME

TO SPAM OR NOT TO SPAM

EMPLOYMENT AND EDUCATION HISTORY DATES

YOUR WAY TO A RESUME

PASSING THE TEST

ONSIDER YOUR RESUME'S ENTRY OINT TO GAIN AN ADVANTAGE

THE IDENTITY THEFT PROBLEM

You've done everything you can to make your resume stand out for the people who'll be deciding your future with the company of your dreams. You've selected a great font arranged in an eye-pleasing layout, and your 24-pound, ecru linen paper stock is the envy of your peers.

But guess what? Nowadays, none of those human touches will matter if you can't get past the computerized systems most HR departments use to screen the thousands of resumes they receive.

At TheLadders, we've evaluated hundreds of thousands of resumes using our proprietary system based on years of research, focus groups with corporate HR departments and executive recruiters, and interviews with the top resume writers in the country.

What have we found? That not everybody needs a professional resume writer to create an effective resume. It turns out that some people hit the mark on their own.

This chapter will address what you'll need to know to write a great resume yourself, and then, later on, how, why, and when to hire a professional resume writer if you don't want to do it yourself.

Either way, here's what you'll get from this chapter:

Your elevator pitch. You'll want to use this succinct statement of your job goals as the basis for writing your resume— make sure that you position your experience, skills and education to support the goals you've set out for yourself.

What are screeners looking for? The first person to look at your resume isn't the person you're going to work for. It's typically an administrative person who combs through databases and applications to find the types of people the hiring manager is looking for.

How to write effectively for keyword search engines. We live in a Google world now, and it's no different with the job search. Making sure that your resume has all the keywords that reflect your expertise and experience is critically important to making sure that the screeners can find you.

Understand the applicant tracking systems used by companies to, well, track all the candidates for their jobs. It's no surprise that companies use software to manage the many resumes they receive.

How to sell your skills to the hiring manager. You're selling the most important product you'll ever sell—the next four or five years of your career. Learn the difference between "telling" and "selling."

Resume, Meet Technology:
How a Machine Reads Your Story

YOU'VE PROBABLY HEARD this advice for making your resume stand out: Sprinkle in plenty of juicy keywords so recruiters will pluck your document out of the pile. But these days, the first review of your resume is more likely to be a software program, known as an Applicant Tracking System (ATS), than a human being interested in the quality of your paper stock and the power of your prose. While those qualities will be important in subsequent rounds, your first challenge will be to win over a very sophisticated machine that plays by its own complex rules.

In competitive times—and to be current regardless of the job market—is a grab bag of keywords really enough to ensure your resume rises out of that mysterious electronic swamp? If not, what else do you need to know? First it's helpful to understand the processes that happen inside these ATSes—systems that are, in fact, fueled by sophisticated data-warehousing technologies—to stand the best chance of getting your resume in front of human eyeballs.

Keywords:
Laundry Lists Don't Cut It

THE ADVICE SIMPLY TO FILL YOUR RESUME with appropriate keywords is becoming outdated. There's a lot more to searching and matching than ever before.

Older ATS software relied on "semantic search" technology that essentially counted keywords. Using a keyword multiple times could improve your score with the ATS if it was programmed to find resumes that featured it, according to Matt Sigelman, CEO of Burning Glass, which makes the search software behind many leading ATS programs. Burning Glass uses "contextualized search," which goes much deeper than a simple keyword count. Instead, it examines factors such as how long ago the applicant acquired the experience they're touting.

State-of-the-art ATS technology, used by more and more companies, relies on contextualization, not on simple keyword matches, agrees Lisa Rowan, program director of human resources, learning and talent strategies for Framingham, Mass.-based analyst firm IDC. "It goes much further, [with the technology looking] at descriptive materials, and [the ATS] parsing things out like a human would when reading it."

With the latest wave of ATS technology, a keyword such as "Java" had "better be framed by descriptive material that demonstrates experience and familiarity with the subject," Rowan warns. This software will examine the entire passage as if it were a human reading your resume: closely and with an understanding of the subject matter.

Resume contextualization analyzes not just a keyword but also its relation to elements, including relevant and related terms, the depth of the experience, and how recent the experience was in a candidate's career path. "Understanding that there's a difference between somebody who took a class in Java eight years ago and somebody who's been programming in Java every day for the last three years—those are fundamentally different candidates," says Sigelman.

Burning Glass' resume-parsing tools seek out far more than keywords or even word strings. For example, instead of just recognizing an employer's name on your resume, Burning Glass technology analyzes the job description to determine your role and what skills correspond to that role.

The keyword laundry list will no longer carry the day, but keywords remain important to the resume and must be included. "Some candidates [for the Java engineering position example] might not write the word 'Java' in their resume, believe it or not," Sieglman says. "I [examined] one job description looking for a geologist. [The candidate's resume listed terms including] water modeling, etc.—all sorts of hydrology [-related terms] and things like that, but never once mentioned the word 'geology' on the resume. The recruiter may have missed this person."

Contextualized resume parsing works to overcome such glaring omissions by understanding the terminology that should surround a word such as "geology." But don't take a chance. There are employers still using primitive semantic search ATSes, so don't skip keywords entirely—just make sure they're positioned in job descriptions that show you can walk the talk.

Don't Choke the ATS

OVERLY FORMATTED RESUMES and resumes embedded with pictures, graphics and logos can be incompatible with most ATS software. Recruiters and human-resources professionals call it "choking the system": An applicant fills his resume with pictures, graphics and logos; headers and footers; and formats that make it difficult for the software to read and sort the text into categories or cause it to crash altogether.

It's a sure way to ensure your resume never makes it to a recruiter, according to Laura Michnya, the project manager of recruiting systems and process for BAE Systems. She recently implemented the Hodes iQ ATS at BAE and in the past has worked with PeopleSoft and several homegrown ATS programs. Some of the resumes she's seen will leave the Hodes iQ system gasping. "Those highly formatted resumes aren't always very compatible with standard ATS systems."

> New resume-parsing tools can understand that there's a difference between somebody who took a class in Java eight years ago and somebody who's been programming in Java every day for the last three years.

Hodes iQ is typical of ATSes, which use software to sift contact information and other chunks of data from uploaded resumes. This makes candidates' resume-uploading experience a little easier, as it pulls that data into a profile instead of forcing them to cut and paste.

But for such parsing software to work properly, a resume needs to be formatted simply. Michnya sees many overly formatted resumes, especially with very senior-level candidates. "A lot of the time, they have so much experience, and they do like to get a little fancy," she says. "And a lot of the time, ATSes don't bring it over cleanly into [the] system."

In some cases, locating contact information in a footer will also cause an ATS to glitch, given that the systems aren't necessarily prepared to expect unusual place-ment. If that same contact information is included in the text, centered at the top of a resume but not in the header, it should come in smoothly, Michnya says. "As long as it's in the body, it will get parsed in fine. But a lot of times people put it just in the header or footer." The result of a highly formatted resume being classified improperly: a garbled mess.

As with graphics, so too with cut-and-pasted text when uploading a resume to a Web site: It's often the cause of ATS choking. That's why Michnya has gone to pains to induce candidates to upload resumes, even switching the order of options on the company's careers site so that the "Upload" option comes first, in big, red text, with the "Cut and Paste" option moved to the bottom of the page.

"If you're on an ATS that gives you the option to either upload or cut and paste into a text box, it's better to upload," she says. "A lot of times that upload feature will parse information for you and will save it in [the optimal] format. It often can save in rich text. If it cuts and pastes, it only does so in plain text, and often people have [their resume] in Word or something that's not plain text," which will lead to the ATS choking and a garbled resume, she says. "With my career site, I find so many candidates do the cut-and-paste option. They think it's faster. But it causes their resume to not look as nice. And hiring managers do notice that."

How to e-Annoy Recruiters Without Really Trying

IT MIGHT SEEM OBVIOUS that capitalization, punctuation and grammar matter. But in the age of shorthand and text messages, mistakes make their way into the resume, says David Freeman, a consultant at Sonic Recruit, a division of Em-eryville, Calif.-based Cytiva Software Inc.

"Especially for Gen Y or Gen X, it's common to type in all lowercase," he says. "They're so used to texting. They're not used to capitalizing anything when texting."

It goes beyond proper etiquette. ATS software uses mail merge to populate fields for e-mails on the applicant to human resources and ultimately to the applicant for follow-up communication. Poor punctuation and capitalization can confuse the software about where to end and begin a field. It also forces the recruiter to enter fields manually, which might lead them to toss your resume.

Another e-annoyance is lag time in responding. Respond swiftly—within 24 hours—to a company that contacts you. Because of the volume of resumes now coming in to recruiters, they're not waiting long to hear back from a candidate.

It's also a good idea to keep an eye on your spam-folder settings. Filters are so sensitive today that they can recognize e-mail that's automatically generated; both spam and follow-up e-mail sent from ATSes fall into this category.

To Spam or Not to Spam

WE ALL KNOW BETTER than to call a hiring manager again and again. But what about pinging the ATS robot accepting your resume again and again? Do duplicate resume submissions hurt your cause? Can it get you noticed?

Jeremy Shapiro, senior vice president of Hodes iQ, believes it hurts your cause. If he could tell applicants one thing, he says, it would be this: "We can see you.

"Recruiters are aware of candidates that send in three different resumes, 10 different resumes," he says. In fact, Shapiro has seen instances of extreme resume spamming, where candidates submit up to 70 to 100 different resumes, all of which are on record in the ATS. "The employer can see it," Shapiro says, and "this does not reflect positively upon [job seekers]."

This is true even in large corporate environments where job seekers may be applying to several different subsidiaries. Even if each division and subsidiary has its own ATS, those systems are usually all linked. But applying for multiple jobs at the same company is not spamming. Just be careful that each resume tells the same story, so as not to raise any red flags.

Consider Your Resume's Entry Point to Gain an Advantage

DO YOU HAVE A BETTER CHANCE at a job if an employee at the company submits your resume? The answer is yes—not only because it influences human screeners but also because of how ATS software follows your resume.

Depending on a given ATS vendor's feature set and how an employer has chosen to set it up, the ATS may track the source of your resume—how it was submitted—and can be designed to attach different values to different sources. An ATS set up to track how resumes come into the system will typically have a source note attached to a resume.

Resumes involved in employee referrals tend to flow into an ATS internally, passed along as a forwarded attachment from the candidate to the referring employee to the recruiter. Even in these circumstances, however, the employer is likely to require that a candidate also fill out an online application.

Most ATSes are sophisticated enough to query how a candidate found out about a job. Employee referrals are one example of applicant sourcing that most employers rank very highly, Rowan notes. If an ATS has ranked Candidate A as being 80 percent qualified, a source note that flags that candidate as also being an employee referral will raise that candidate's ranking.

"If I'm an employee, I'm not going to recommend poor candidates, generally. So they're thought to be higher quality," Rowan says.

Other examples are Web sites, job boards and recruiters. Was the candidate's resume found on a niche job board, for example, that features the resumes of minorities? Some employers, such as one requesting federal contract work, might program the ATS to assign a higher value to such a resume. Job boards and recruiters with a particularly good reputation with an employer might also earn a few extra points for a submitted resume.

The lesson is simple: If you are in fact being referred by an employee, make sure the ATS knows it—because it's smart enough to care.

The Bottom Line on Applicant Tracking Systems

INSIGHTS INTO ATS TECHNOLOGY are helpful and can help you avoid missing keywords and choking the software, but there is no way to game the systems. Don't even try. Best practice simply ensures you won't be disqualified for a technical error. But resumes still touch human hands and must be optimized for the reader as well.

The human element still carries the day, particularly when it comes to the importance of letting peers review your resume before it ever reaches an ATS. "A great person may not have a great resume," Shapiro of Hodes iQ says. "Circulate your resume to peers, and to friends, before you send it off. Make sure little mistakes are gone. And make sure it's pleasant to look through."

Think about it this way: Your resume is the first writing sample your prospective employer ever sees. This is an opportunity to blow it or impress. Keeping it simple, concise and clear will not only help it pass through the ATS gauntlet—it will provide your prospective employer his first chance to evaluate what you're made of.

To Tell the Truth

THE WOMAN WAS MOUSY AND SMALL, just 5 feet tall and 105 pounds. She wanted to be hired full time at the Ohio-based manufacturing facility where she was temping, and asked what she had to do to make that happen.

"Well, you have to fill out an application and go through an interview, and then we'll do a background check," the vice president of human resources, Matthew Rosen, told her.

"I'll have a tough time with the background check," said the woman.

That was an understatement. The background check revealed a criminal record and hard time in a penitentiary. When Rosen asked the woman about it, she said her husband had beaten her, repeatedly. So she shot him—a crime for which she spent seven years behind bars.

Rosen's jaw hit the floor. And yet, he recommended hiring her. It "turned out beautifully," Rosen remembers. The woman is still working at the plant today. She's one of the organization's best workers, grateful to have been given a chance. It's an extreme case, but many people have issues they'd rather sweep under the carpet than reveal on a resume—from work-history gaps to degrees not received to an age that's either too ripe or too raw to admit. But all resume issues have one thing in common: Getting caught in a lie about them can obliterate your chances of getting hired. "It's going to be discovered," believes Rosen. And then, "There will be no chance you'll get that job.

"You have a better chance explaining it—much better. If they run a background check, then it will get discovered, and then you've lied to these people. Who'll hire someone who's lied to them? I'm going to hire someone who did something and went to a penitentiary. I'll never hire someone who's lied to me."

But while it's easy to preach truthfulness, resumes are marketing documents that present candidates in the best light. You need to ask yourself: What can you successfully gloss over, and how do you do it without turning yourself into a liar? In other words, when is it all right to polish, and when does an embellishment become a forgery?

It's crucial to understand the difference between an appropriate omission and a deliberate disguise. The next section explains how to make each part of your resume shine and still stay within the bounds of honesty. The result is a clear topography of this slippery slope for all those job seekers who've found they question the distinction between exaggeration and fabrication.

Where Does Your Resume Go?

WHAT HAPPENS TO YOUR RESUME after you hit "Submit"? Knowing the technical journey it takes can be essential to impressing the recruiter and scoring an interview. Almost all resumes these days enter an Applicant Tracking System, where they're sorted, categorized and stored. It's the ATS that analyzes each resume before choosing which ones to forward to the human hands of a recruiter. While each ATS works a little differently, the flowchart (below and on the following pages) tracks the basic steps and provides useful know-how whether you're starting to write your resume from square one, giving it a tuneup or making some final tweaks.

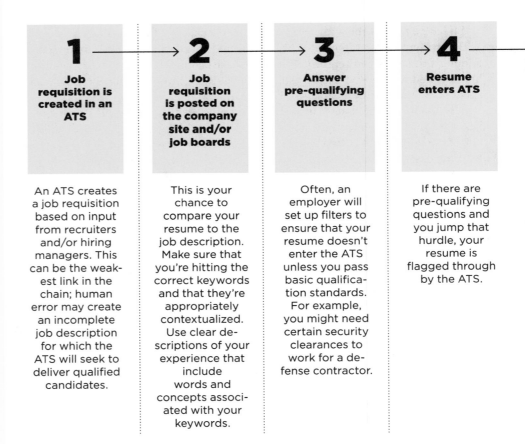

1
Job requisition is created in an ATS

An ATS creates a job requisition based on input from recruiters and/or hiring managers. This can be the weakest link in the chain; human error may create an incomplete job description for which the ATS will seek to deliver qualified candidates.

2
Job requisition is posted on the company site and/or job boards

This is your chance to compare your resume to the job description. Make sure that you're hitting the correct keywords and that they're appropriately contextualized. Use clear descriptions of your experience that include words and concepts associated with your keywords.

3
Answer pre-qualifying questions

Often, an employer will set up filters to ensure that your resume doesn't enter the ATS unless you pass basic qualification standards. For example, you might need certain security clearances to work for a defense contractor.

4
Resume enters ATS

If there are pre-qualifying questions and you jump that hurdle, your resume is flagged through by the ATS.

5

ATS categorizes chunks of information

Advanced ATSes, such as those powered by Burning Glass technology, categorize pieces of your resume. Imagine stickies affixed to each piece of information, all of which are, in Burning Glass' case, tagged for the software to sort.

6

Advanced ATSes learn from your resume

The ATSes from some vendors will have learned from past resume parsing how to detect patterns. Instead of relying on its users to give it a script of what a resume looks like and a set of rules for how to interpret that information, an advanced ATS can, at this point, make judgment calls as to whether, for example, a phone number pertains to the job candidate or to a person listed as a reference, or whether the job candidate attended the University of Michigan or worked there instead.

7

Advanced ATSes compare your resume with those of others

An advanced ATS will evaluate your career path and predict what your next logical job might be so that it can evaluate your experiences and skills within the context of a logical career trajectory. If you're a vice president in charge of human resources, for example, applying for a job as an entry-level recruiter doesn't make sense for your career trajectory.

8

Advanced ATSes evaluate other filter elements

An employer may want to interpret your address, for example, to determine if you live within a given radius of its work site.

9
Resumes are ranked

Some ATS software will, at this point, affix a score to your resume. Recruiters or hiring managers will choose whether to take a closer look at, say, the top 10 percent or 20 percent.

10
Points are added to resumes referred by high-quality sources

If an employer has chosen to track the source of a resume, a field will be attached for that purpose. Some ATS software will increase a resume's ranking if, for example, that resume comes from a referring employee or a trusted recruiter.

11
Duplicate resumes are archived together

This technique varies from employer to employer and from ATS to ATS. Typically, duplicate resumes will all be attached to the same candidate. Recruiters will be able to discern at a glance how many times you've applied and can compare your resumes to see whether there are serious discrepancies or if you've simply tweaked your resume to apply to different jobs, which they recognize as a legitimate cause for multiple resume submissions.

12a
Contact is initiated

If the hiring manager or recruiter decides to follow through, whether to ask more questions or invite you to an interview, many ATSes will use your name and contact information from your resume to pre-populate the initial e-mail.

12b
Or ... "We'll keep your resume on file"

This used to mean a dusty metal filing cabinet. ATSes now offer powerful databases that employers use to search for candidates before a job requisition even makes it to job boards or the company's recruiting site.

Employment and Education History Dates

IT'S A BAD IDEA to fudge dates, given how easy it is to check dates of employment and graduation. But with age discrimination at both ends of the experience spectrum, there's sound justification for strategically dealing with dates—in particular, dates of college graduation. "For some jobs, like those of top executives, employers won't hire [somebody] in his early 30s," says Steve Burdan, a certified professional resume writer who works with TheLadders. "They're looking for [an applicant] in his 40s or early 50s."

Similarly, applicants in their 50s can face prejudice toward older workers and their presumed inflexibility regarding salary, learning new technology or being managed by a younger person.

BOTTOM LINE:
- It is acceptable to omit graduation dates, but it can lead recruiters to think you are trying to mask your age.
- Every position must include the year but not the month.

When to Date Yourself

BURDAN WAS ONCE A RECRUITER and admits that checking on college dates is the first thing he'd do when reviewing an application. "I'd take the resume and go immediately to the college [dates] to figure out how old they are," he says.

Now that he's a resume writer, Burdan handles resume dates differently depending on where a job seeker is in her career path. If a candidate has had only three jobs in her career and received a degree in 1988, Burdan will include the college dates to signal how old the subject is. If the subject is in his early 60s or 70s, Burdan excludes college dates completely.

The point isn't to lie, Burdan says; the point is to "throw [employers] off the trail as long as possible." An employer will eventually find out a candidate's age. But the longer it takes for that to happen, the less time there is for that employer to rule somebody out due to preconceptions about their age, and the more time there is for a candidate to get into an interview and build a relationship with her interviewers.

But be forewarned: Recruiters know what you're up to when you're cagey with dates, and leaving them out can set off alarms. "Dates [are] something critical to have on your resume," says Jacqueline Hudson, a senior account executive for the Renascent Group LLC, an executive search firm. "I totally understand age discrimination, but [if dates aren't included] automatically [a recruiter will think], 'What are they hiding? Are they too junior or are they too senior?' "

Dates of Employment and Work History

WHILE LEAVING OFF EDUCATION DATES clearly has its pluses and minuses, leaving off work-history dates is never a good idea. Recruiters like to see how long a candidate stayed with an employer and, specifically, how many years of experience he or she had in a given role. "If they list five jobs with no dates, we don't know if they spent 25 years at one job and one with another," Hudson says. "[Dates] show consistency and what your [work history] pattern is. Nobody wants to hire somebody who will turn around and work for someone else in less than a year." For those worried about a short tenure at a job, contemporary wisdom dictates eliminating months and including only years for job-history dates.

If you began your professional career in 1974, are you required to fill several pages with jobs, promotions and duties dating back 35 years?

No. Convention in the resume industry—which is driven largely by the expectations of recruiters and hiring managers—dictates that candidates include the past 10 to 12 years of work history on their resumes.

Job seekers typically feel compelled to list every single thing they've done since they started their professional careers. But most recruiters and hiring managers don't care to go back that far, and exhaustive detail is unnecessary.

Use discretion to cull work history beyond the 12-year mark. If a job held more than 12 years ago seems relevant to the position you're applying for, it's acceptable to include the employer, job title and dates of employment without a full job description. Just be prepared to explain why this experience is relevant.

Mind the Gaps

LYING BY OMISSION OCCURS in the work-history section when candidates exclude or try to hide employment gaps. Hiring professionals are trained to spot such gaps or to weed them out in background checks, and they'll typically assume that a candidate is trying to hide something if they find an unexplained gap.

Gaps can have myriad legitimate reasons: Examples include a retirement that was cut short due to a nose-diving 401(k) plan, childbirth or family issues, a sabbatical, or a return to school to pursue a degree. Candidates often write what's known as a "functional" resume to try to cover up such gaps. In a functional resume, company names and job accomplishments are provided without dates.

Be careful. When looking at a functional resume, hiring professionals can't tell when or where a given accomplishment happened, and it may suggest that a job seeker is trying to hide something. Right off the bat, you might give someone cause for worry, and if they're worried enough, you could put yourself out of contention.

BOTTOM LINE:
- It is acceptable to omit work experience, or limit details, after 10 to 12 years.
- Don't cover gaps by extending your tenure at previous positions.
- Fill in gaps with consulting and volunteer positions or list the reasons for the unemployment.

Be forthright by documenting all work-history gaps just as you would a job. For

CAUGHT LYING

Recruiters and hiring professionals share some of the whoppers and doozies job seekers have tried to sneak into resumes over the years.

48-hour promotion
"I once got two resumes a couple of days apart from the same candidate—[who was] applying for different jobs. The dates of employment and some of the areas of responsibility were changed in the second resume. And she must have had a promotion in the past 48 hours because the second resume showed a new manager title at her current job!"
—*David Lewis*

¿Habla español?
"I have started out interviews speaking in Spanish when the resume claims fluency, only to discover that the individual never got beyond the basics and I lost them at 'Hola.' "
—*Christine Bolzan*

10 credits shy
"An investment-banking client sent us a candidate for our outplacement program. Human resources discovered, quite by accident, that the employee had not received his Bachelor's Degree, as he had listed on his resume. The truth was he was 10 credits shy of earning a degree. The company had a policy that if an employee had lied on his resume, the person had to be released. Everyone at the company was heartbroken, as this was a generally beloved employee, but they had to [follow the] letter of the law."
—*Sally Haver*

Fake references
"[Some candidates] substitute the name of a company friend for that of their immediate superior. Call to check the reference, and the friend tells you the candidate is a cross between Jack Welch and Mother Teresa. That's when the fun begins, especially if the candidate wasn't smart enough to send the friend a copy of the resume. The friend is willing to vouch for anything, but they can never be completely sure of the fabricated details. 'So you can verify the candidate made $250,000 their last full year there?' I'll ask, looking at the line on the resume that claims he made $150,000. 'It was right around there,' the friend says, thinking he's being cagey. 'Maybe a few dollars more, a few dollars less, but in that ballpark.' I make up a couple more 'facts' the friend is happy to swear to, and then move on to the next candidate."
—*Barry Maher*

example, if you took a sabbatical from 2001 to 2003, include that information on your resume, with "sabbatical" in all capital and/or bold letters, just as if it were a company name. That way, the gap is right up front, addressed and filled in for the hiring manager who's just looking at the dates. It gets you through the human-resources screen, but you won't be accused of trying to hide anything. And in to-day's environment, "a lot of people have gaps on their resumes," says Stephen Van Vreede, a resume writer who works with TheLadders.

Case in point: Schiller International University's Rosen reviewed a resume in mid-July that included a gap in employment, but the applicant had been clear that the gap was due to time spent as a stay-at-home mother. "Well, that's fine," Rosen says. "That was explained." Another easily explained gap is having been laid off. "These days, losing a job is not a black eye anymore. At one point, if you got laid

4 THINGS YOU MUST KNOW ABOUT PRE-HIRE TESTS

PRE-HIRE SCREENING TESTS have long been a common presence in big-box stores, where job applicants sit at a little booth near the front door for a quick test to determine if they're suitable even to apply. The technique is not typically associated with $100K+ jobs—but that is changing. Employers are beginning to mandate applicants take an online pre-hire assessment test as they submit their resume, and it can determine whether your resume even makes it to Step One of the application process. Here's what to be aware of:

1. **Pre-hire assessment tests examine your skill level** and whether or not you would fit into the cultural and ethical environment of the employer. It measures your answers against what the employer has defined as the profile of an ideal employee in that position. The test is psycho-

metric, testing personality and style as opposed to skills. It's also subjective: for a sales position, it may reflect a particular sales style a given employer prefers and assess how a candidate thinks and behaves to determine if he would be a good fit.

2. **Rapid (and expensive) employee turnover rates motivated retailers' embrace of pre-hire assessment tests,** but their use has percolated upward into companies searching to fill higher-level sales positions. And shrinking human-resources departments and the surge in applicants has fueled demand for an early screening.

3. **There are no right or wrong answers on psychometric tests.** For skills tests, job seekers can self-test using tools on Monster, for example.

Otherwise, make sure you answer pre-screening questions accurately if you want your resume to make it into an employer's ATS.

4. **The pre-hire test is as important as your resume.** "People think, 'I've got the keywords, yadda, yadda, yadda.' Well, the game starts with the screening questions," says Chris Forman, chief development officer and president of AIRS, a recruitment outsourcer. "If you answer it wrong, or answer it right and you're not what they're looking for, your resume will get knocked out.

"There's this belief that the resume is what will put you at the top of the list. That's the case in a number of companies, but more and more today, it's those knockout questions that will tag you as qualified or unqualified."

off, people thought there was something wrong with you," Rosen says. "Nowadays if you lose your job, it's no big deal."

Rosen is also understanding about work histories that are somewhat inconsistent, as long as the inconsistencies are explainable. He talked to another job seeker recently who had been at one job for a long time, followed by short tenures at two companies—a potential red flag from a recruiter's perspective. The candidate explained that he had moved on from the long-term position to a new one but left because of a disagreement with a supervisor. He had then moved into a position in the mortgage industry but lost his job in the early days of the recession. "That's OK," Rosen says. "They were at one job for 18, 20 years—that's OK. That's a reasonable explanation."

Van Vreede and Burdan recommend that job seekers fill in gaps on their resumes resulting from layoffs with any consulting, freelance or contract work completed. Include pro bono or volunteer work as well. For those who have done nothing since losing a job, putting nothing down can work if there have been only a few months of downtime. If you've done nothing for more than six months, you're getting to the point where people will start to worry. However, unemployment remains common enough in this economy that it should not automatically disqualify a job seeker.

The point isn't to lie about your age. The point is to throw employers off the trail as long as possible.

Job Titles

INSERT THE OFFICIAL TITLE[S] used by your previous employer[s] on your resume. When it comes to job titles, there is no way around the truth. You must always be honest because titles are easily verified by reference and background checks. "By default, you should provide the title referred to by the employer," explains Burdan.

"Companies like the Big Five, they'll have titles like 'senior auditor.' You have to go along with that," he says, even if that title has an unclear meaning out of context. "That's what the industry knows and the company uses. It's awkward, but you've got to use it."

Exceptions to the Rule

THERE IS, HOWEVER, SOME WIGGLE ROOM. An acceptable title change, for example, would be for an applicant who was both a sales representative and a manager. If that job seeker decides he wants to do only sales and would rather not manage anymore, it's permissible to include only the sales experience on his resume. Job seekers who were business owners present a particular problem for Burdan. Too often they include inflated titles, such as "president and CEO," he says. He advises against those titles, even if that's what the individual's business card says. Instead, he advises using a title such as "principal."

The rationale boils down to perception: There's a big difference between being the president of a one-person company and being the president of General Electric. In most cases, it's wise to dial it back to avoid being seen as exaggerating your role, Burdan advises.

Burdan also suggests translating or converting titles of candidates who have military or government experience. Titles such as "colonel," "major" or "agent in charge" don't have clear meaning within the business community.

Education

ACCU-SCREEN, a company that specializes in employment background checks, has found during the course of tracking 15 years' worth of screens that some 16 percent of academic degrees and institutions listed on resumes are falsified. Job seekers also falsify 15 percent of technical skills and certifications, Accu-Screen has found.

Many job candidates who have gone to college but haven't graduated lie by saying that they've completed a degree. Resume writers also often find such candidates using qualifying language such as "only four credits left to get a Bachelor of Science degree."

Both tactics are "huge mistakes," cautions Van Vreede. "Any reasonable person will look at the candidate and say, 'Are you stupid? Why didn't you go back and finish your degree? Take correspondence courses online. What are you waiting for?' " And perhaps even more to the point, language tricks send up red flags, giving the impression that a job seeker is trying to be sneaky. A better approach than lying or manipulating language is to say that you attended a program or did coursework at a particular institution. Here's another technique that resume writer Burdan uses: For those who have college degrees, he labels the section "Education." For those who lack degrees, he bundles their education up in a section he labels "Professional Training."

In a Professional Training section, you can state, for example, that you've completed three years of a Bachelor of Science in finance program at the University of Georgia. By labeling it "Professional Training," it appears less like an aborted degree and more like continuing education. After all, many people churn through a boatload of seminars and workshops above and beyond their formal education, Burdan notes.

Certifications

TECHNICAL CERTIFICATIONS represent a special case. The technology industry is a field in which it is common to find faked certifications. Many IT job candidates will load their resumes with certificate lists or even paste in graphics that only certificate holders have the right to use—such as an MCSE (Microsoft Certified Systems Engineer) credential—thinking they won't be checked.

But faking certifications, professional accreditations, trade memberships or professional licenses is a cardinal sin because it's very easy to check with the organizations that award the titles, and the hiring companies often face liability for hiring someone who faked an accreditation.

GPA

ANOTHER EDUCATION-RELATED LIE TO AVOID: fudging your grade point average. Christine Bolzan, CEO of Graduate Career Coaching, says that job seekers often exaggerate GPAs but that even the slightest tweak will raise a red flag. "In today's job market, you can't create any type of question about your candidacy," she says.

"[Employers] want highly ethical individuals, and hiring companies have their pick. You might say you have a 3.8 GPA and it comes back as a 3.78 GPA. That will raise the red flag. The candidate will say, 'I was just rounding up,' but with the job market as competitive as it is now, there's no room for rounding up."

BOTTOM LINE:
- Never claim a degree or certificate you do not possess.
- Never falsify or round up a GPA.

Avoiding Temptation

THINKING OF PADDING YOUR RESUME to increase your chance of landing a job? Here's some advice: Think again. History is littered with names such as these: George O'Leary, former football coach for Notre Dame, fired in 2001 after only five days on the job for lying on his resume about a Master's Degree he never earned and an exaggerated position on the University of New Hampshire football team; Sandra Baldwin, former president of the United States Olympic Committee, who

> There's a big difference between being the president of a one-person company and being the president of General Electric. In most cases, it's wise to dial it back so as to avoid being seen as an exaggerator.

resigned in 2002 when a reporter revealed she never earned the Doctoral Degree she claimed on her resume.

Many job seekers are tempted to stretch the truth on their resumes, claiming degrees that they never completed, job responsibilities that are questionable and additional years of tenure they pull from thin air.

A recent survey of business owners by online payroll provider Sure Payroll shows just how common the practice is:

- 21 percent of respondents reported hiring dishonest employees.
- 47 percent of respondents said a job seeker who lied in an interview caused the hiring mistake.
- 79 percent said they had hired employees with mismatched skill sets or who displayed underperformance on the job, despite the claims made on their resume.

For the hiring company, the mistake can be expensive: Forty-eight percent of business owners told Sure Payroll those bad hires cost them more than $1,000, and 9 percent said losses exceeded $10,000. A deceitful or exaggerated resume can devastate someone's chances of getting hired or staying hired, since every detail on a resume can (and likely will) be verified.

In a Google World, Prepare to Be Investigated

HOW LIKELY IS IT THAT YOUR RESUME, job application and credentials will be reviewed for inaccuracies? Nearly 100 percent, according to the Society for Human Resource Management. Almost all human resources professionals reported to SHRM that their organizations conduct some form of background check on every employee. For some candidates, it doesn't take much more than a Google search to pull up information, both good and bad.

Besides seeing things like what you have published, an online search can also reveal unflattering or downright negative things someone may have said about you. Beyond that, most recruiters check references at every company you list to verify your duties, tenure, salary, and in some cases even your W2. Their findings include the most damning documentation, including police reports, articles about misconduct and more. All that information is shared with the recruiters' client: the hiring manager.

If you have been interviewed and a falsification is uncovered, chances are that's the end of the road for that job and possibly future opportunities as well. It will be disheartening to you in your job search and cost you potentially useful contacts, so think long and hard if you feel tempted to lie.

Stretching the Truth

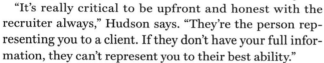

MORE OFTEN THAN NOT, a dishonest resume is not an outright lie but a truth stretched too far. Besides exaggerating salary, many candidates will exaggerate their experience, responsibilities and duties. For example, candidates who want to get into marketing but who have experience in sales will often puff up their resume to make it appear that they have much more marketing experience than they actually do. Stretching the truth in this way isn't necessarily fraudulent, but it's a waste of time. HR pros and recruiters will get to the truth at some point, and you will likely be disqualified from consideration for the job.

"It's really critical to be upfront and honest with the recruiter always," Hudson says. "They're the person representing you to a client. If they don't have your full information, they can't represent you to their best ability."

Before you reach the point where you're stretching the truth, focus carefully on the positions for which you're applying, making sure a given job is a good fit all the way around, not just because it's at the director level, for example. If it's a good fit, as it should be, there's just no reason to stretch the truth. Your real qualifications will speak for themselves.

TOP 3 REASONS NOT TO LIE

1. If you are caught lying it is too hard to keep lies covered, and, when ultimately caught, your chances of being hired are all but obliterated.

2. The Internet and background checks make it hard to cover up a lie.

3. Even exaggerations can hurt you in a tough employment market.

The Identity-Theft Problem

LET'S FACE IT: A job search is not easy on introverts. The whole process of polishing up your personal brand and putting it on the open market is an exercise in self-exposure that can test the nerve of even the most outgoing candidate.

In a market saturated with job seekers, a battery of software and human gatekeepers will scrutinize the personal information you provide. The more opportunities you pursue, the more places that data will travel.

And in this age of identity theft and data piracy, that raises the chances that your information will take a bad turn and end up in the wrong hands. On this planet, there's no absolute guarantee of data security; nevertheless, understanding the threat and using some precautions should make your job search both successful and secure.

Consider this case in point.

"Proper storage of employee and applicant records." It was just another item on the human resources audit checklist, right after "display federal, state and OSHA labor law posters." After checking off a few other items on her checklist, Ellen B. Vance, an HR consultant and auditor, asked to see the storage room. The client led her to an unlocked storage closet in the middle of the old building, surrounded by half of the nonprofit's 40 employees.

When she opened the door, Vance encountered 15 large file-folder boxes. "When we moved to this new location, we just put this stuff in there," said the client.

Vance and the client started opening boxes. As they did, it became clear that "this stuff" included photocopies of birth certificates; Social Security cards; driver's licenses; and I-9 Employment Eligibility Verification forms that listed employees' Social Security numbers, dates of birth, addresses, maiden names, signatures—everything a criminal needs to perpetrate identity theft. "I was about ready to pass out, seeing all this stuff," says Vance.

DATA THEFT: WHERE COMPANIES LEAK

WHAT DID THEY TAKE?

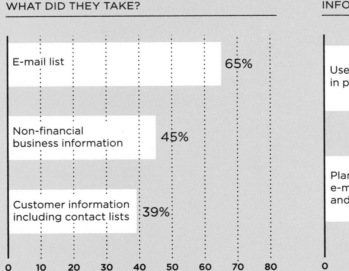

E-mail list	65%
Non-financial business information	45%
Customer information including contact lists	39%

WHAT DID THEY DO WITH THE CONFIDENTIAL INFORMATION THEY LIFTED?

Used confidential information in pursuit of a new job	67%
Planned to use stolen data from e-mail lists, customer contact lists and employee records	68%

Source: Data Loss Risks During Downsizing, Ponemon Institute LLC

Why should you care about the poor compliance procedures at a nonprofit in Virginia? If you've applied to a job there or anywhere in the last decade, your resume may be equally exposed, your personal information similarly vulnerable to identity theft should anyone gain access to an unlocked closet and a stack of file folders. With the advent of e-mailed resumes, electronic storage and online applications, the thief need not even get so close; your resume may be open to attack from an unscrupulous recruiter or hacker.

Too few companies employ the safeguards necessary to protect applicant data, and almost none inform clients of their security practices before requesting resume and applicant information. The economy has made matters somewhat worse, according to HR managers, who say the employers' market has left job seekers feeling compelled to hand over information they would normally be reluctant to reveal and distribute it to dozens of sources in the hopes of finding a job. Criminals have even been known to post fake job listings to capture the data of unsuspecting job seekers.

Fumbled Data

INTERVIEWS WITH HIRING PROFESSIONALS confirm the anecdotal evidence: Even recruiting agencies that use sophisticated ATS software to store and protect job applications often leave the applications open to theft by allowing access to anybody and everybody who walks by an unsecured terminal; companies leave sensitive information moldering in unlocked closets accessible to all; and job applicants' data gets left on laptops that get stolen and on USB thumb drives that get misplaced.

In her experience, Vance says that small firms without formal HR departments are most likely to fumble data. But make no mistake: Large corporations with entrenched HR processes are still liable to mishandle job-applicant or employee data. Two recent examples include Aetna and the Gap. The U.S. insurance giant was sued after allegedly failing to protect personal information belonging to employees and job applicants. This was direct fallout from an incident in which the company's job-application Web site was breached by cyber criminals, as Aetna disclosed. For its part, the Gap lost personal information, including Social Security numbers, for some 800,000 U.S. and Canadian job seekers.

But help is on the way: Employers are on notice to improve resume data protection after data breaches precipitated several lawsuits and government action. What's more, job seekers can implement their own safeguards to avoid putting their resume in the wrong hands (See 5 Ways to Protect Your Resume from Identity Theft, page 79).

Can We Blame the ATS?

JOB-APPLICATION INFORMATION is walking out the door in a number of ways, but often, insecure software is to blame. Research firm Forrester Research recently found that more than 62 percent of 200 surveyed companies experienced a security breach in the previous 12 months because of insecure software. Most were likely caused by an SQL injection attack.

In an SQL injection, a hacker uses a Web site's online form to gain control of the database. Security procedures are designed to filter and block such attacks, but hackers are constantly developing new codes and techniques and almost no database is safe, says a security analyst who works for one of the major ATS vendors.

"If you have an application publicly available on the Internet with form fields, people could potentially execute database statements if proper input filtering is not performed," says the analyst, who asked not to be identified.

How do ATS vendors fend off an SQL injection? According to our source, his company uses filters to prevent an SQL injection and XSS (cross-site scripting) to find and patch vulnerable code in the database software. The ATS vendor monitors activity logs for such types of attempted breaches against its Web-based applicant tracking and performance management software. In addition, the ATS vendor stores the resumes and applicant data for its clients at its own facility; only two people—the vendor's CEO and the security analyst himself—have physical access to servers that are accessed via biometric palm-print recognition.

Stretching the truth on your resume isn't necessarily fraudulent, but it's a waste of time. At some point, you will be exposed and then likely disqualified from consideration.

A People Problem

BUT TECHNOLOGY IS ONLY PART OF THE PROBLEM. All the software in the world won't protect applicant data if humans handle the technology recklessly.

Rachel Rice-Haase, human-resources and marketing coordinator for Oberstadt Landscapes & Nursery Inc. in Fremont, Wis., has witnessed that recklessness firsthand. In a previous position at a recruiting company, recruiters used an ATS that Rice-Haase called "pretty up to date" to process applications. The company's help desk made sure to give tutorials to recruiters so they knew how to use the ATS applications. It all seemed "pretty advanced," Rice-Haase explains. The software probably was sophisticated when it came to security and features, but the more she looked at it, the more Rice-Haase realized the company was using it carelessly.

"You had anybody, even people who weren't recruiters, going in and accessing applicants' information," she says. "You might have 10 recruiters, and they all have access to everybody's candidates. It's not just people you've interviewed. It's the person sitting across from you, down the hall, [they] can get in there and look at [any job applicant's information]. That part was always baffling to me. Sure, you sign a little form saying, 'I won't take this information home with me.' But you have to wonder, when all this information is available to everybody at the recruiting center, how far that goes?"

It can go pretty far. As Rice-Haase describes it, the ATS collected information including Social Security number, date of birth, driver's license number—"all this stuff you'd rather not have anybody and everybody have access to," she says, and that's typical of ATS software.

With the software, recruiters could create a resume for any candidate and e-mail it from the system. Convenient? Yes. Dangerous? Absolutely. Recruiters could e-mail out personal information or entire applications.

And sometimes a company doesn't have a clue—or perhaps doesn't much care—where its data is stored or how to prevent loss. The Virginia company with the unlocked storage room is another classic example of blissful ignorance: Even though the company is legally responsible for safekeeping of the confidential information stored on I-9 forms, the staff just didn't know what was in those 15 boxes.

Vance encouraged her client to go through the files, pull out the forms, put them into a shredder, and to have a witness on hand to make sure the records were verifiably demolished. "She looked at me with a look of horror on her face," Vance says. "[She was] staring at these boxes. She didn't know how many contained employee files, so she had to go through all of them. It was one of those cases where they didn't know what they didn't know. They didn't have an HR person there to advise them on it."

A Technology Solution

MANY ORGANIZATIONS FAIL TO GRASP the scope of data protection or understand that it goes beyond the technology, says Jenny Yang, senior manager of product marketing for data-loss prevention at Symantec, a security-technology company. They don't understand:

- Where the confidential data is
- Where it's going and how it's moving—for example, is it being e-mailed out as part of a monthly report to the vice president of human resources, or is it being casually e-mailed around by recruiters, as was done at Rice-Haase's former recruiting agency employer?
- How to prevent it from leaving an organization

Companies like Symantec provide some technology solutions to the problem of managers who mishandle applicant data. Symantec makes a product that searches a company's entire network for sensitive data, like Social Security numbers, even if it's on a USB memory stick attached to someone's laptop. It will also ID and block such data from being transmitted outside the company's network, either by a negligent employee or a hacker. But such software won't help job seekers unless all potential employers have opted to buy it, and few companies will tell applicants whether they use such technology.

Unlike e-commerce sites, which advertise their security practices to gain the trust of consumers about to hand over credit card data, few employers advertise the steps they take to protect your resume and job application. To protect your resume and sensitive data, the best practice, for now, Vance says, is to make less of it available.

Recruiters don't have time to read your life story. Resumes should include only the info relevant to the job or your work history.

8 Ways Your Resume Can Say "I'm Unprofessional"

NO OFFENSE, thebigcheese@domain.com, but if nobody has mentioned it yet, we're mentioning it now: That e-mail address is not making you look particularly professional.

Wacky e-mail addresses are just one way of sending hiring managers the wrong message. If you want to be taken seriously when you apply for jobs, you need to put some polish on your resume, your cover letter and everything contained therein. Hiring professionals repeatedly run across these red flags that scream "unprofessional." Below, some common faux pas.

1. Random/cute/shared e-mail accounts

E-mail accounts are free. There's no reason not to sign up for your own. Yet many mid-career professionals share an e-mail account with a significant other or the entire family, generating addresses such as dickandjane@domain.com or thesmiths@domain.com.

Also stay away from cutesy addresses. After all, butterfliesaremyfriend2010@domain.com, you can always share your admiration of *Lepidoptera* with colleagues after you've been hired. Ditto for offensive, flirtatious or sexual e-mail addresses.

Instead, adopt an address that incorporates the name you use professionally on your resume and cover letter.

2. Failure to proofread

Deidre Pannazzo, executive director at Inspired Resumes, says it's "amazing" how many people submit resumes that contain "numerous typos and misspellings." You've heard it before, but we can't emphasize it enough: proofread, proofread, proofread.

3. Bikini pictures

Resume experts advise against attaching pictures or any image files to a resume. They can "choke" an ATS, the software that automatically scans and parses resumes. In addition, hiring professionals warn against giving anyone a reason to prejudge and form a negative opinion based on your appearance. Indeed, some HR departments will immediately discard resumes with photos to avoid any possible accusations of discrimination on this basis. Despite this conventional wisdom, many applicants still send photos. Most troublesome of all, says Jillian Zavitz, program manager at TalktoCanada.com, are the beach shots. "[No] pictures where you are in a bikini at the beach (real story, and it wasn't a flattering picture either) or at a New Year's party with your friends (obviously drunk). Not cool."

4. Unprofessional voicemail

If your resume is strong enough to convince the recruiter or hiring manager to reach for the telephone, be sure what he finds at the other end of the line represents you in the best light— that means your voicemail or whoever might answer the phone. Marlane Perry, managing director of the executive search division of Magill Associates, says she is unimpressed when a phone number on a resume leads her to an unprofessional recorded voicemail or a conversation with a third party who can't be trusted to take a message. "If you don't trust your roommates to answer the phone and take a decent message, then only list your cell phone," she says.

5. Lazy words, "Etc."

Perry says that among her pet peeves is the use of "etc." on a resume. She believes it is indicative of laziness: The job seeker obviously "can't even take the time to list out all of [her] duties." She has seen the error on both junior- and executive-level resumes. Another no-no is saying "same as above" anywhere on a resume. "If you had similar job

5 WAYS TO PROTECT YOUR RESUME FROM IDENTITY THEFT

1. Before receiving a job offer, omit any fields on forms that ask for sensitive information such as Social Security number, driver's license or maiden name. A prospective employer does not need that data.

2. Leave your home address off your cover letter and resume. Most communication is by e-mail and phone, so this shouldn't raise any red flags.

3. Avoid unmonitored sites, such as Craigslist. Instead, use reputable sites that identify the company posting the listing. If you're not sure whether it's a bona fide listing, send a request for additional information.

4. Use a separate e-mail account for your job search so you can isolate your e-mail, both for security purposes and to keep track of job correspondence.

5. Once a job offer comes, avoid providing copies of documents used for I-9 purposes, such as passports or birth certificates. Employers can legally record the documents' information, but don't hand over photocopies that can be mishandled.

functions at your last two jobs, summarize the responsibilities and then bullet out some of your accomplishments," she suggests.

6. Cookie-cutter resumes

Samantha Goldberg is a celebrity event designer and TV personality who's always looking for employees for administrative duties or to help plan an event. She says she often reviews resumes and cover letters that aren't even vaguely customized for her business.

"It's more like 'Mad Libs'—they just fill in our name as they send them off!" she says. "Just once, I would love to have them describe me on the cover letter instead of saying that they respect my career status and have been following my career."

On many occasions, Goldberg says, she specifically lists a prerequisite of at least three years' experience with planning events that does not include friends, family or one's own weddings. "They obviously don't read my prerequisites and send an e-mail stating that even though they haven't orchestrated events for anyone, they have always been told they should be in the industry if I would just give them a chance."

7. Everything but the kitchen sink

"I don't care, nor have time, to read about your life story," Zavitz says. "If you can't whittle your resume down to a page or two max, I will not read it. If it's not related [to the job or your work history], don't include it."

8. Ad infinitum ...

Larry Lambeth, president of Employment Screening Services Inc., which helps companies review job applicants, offers a laundry list of professional gaffes he's seen on resumes and job applications:
- Listing a spouse as a reference
- Not spelling out the name of an employer or school ("LSU" instead of "Louisiana State University" or "ZDE" instead of "Ziff Davis Enterprise")
- Not providing a city or state for an employer or school
- Omitting the area code from a phone number
- Providing only a first name for a supervisor or reference
- Including phone numbers that are no longer in service

> **Professional resume writers have abandoned the objective statement for an executive summary aimed at needs of the employer.**

Negotiate a Bigger Salary With Your Resume

SHE WAS PERFECT FOR THE JOB. She had experience teaching both online and in the Middle East, she was available to work immediately, and she had a Master's Degree in Teaching English to Speakers of Other Languages (TESOL).

She was so perfect, the hiring company, TalktoCanada.com, the online English language-training company, was prepared to offer her 20 percent more than the typical starting salary, according to program manager Zavitz.

Most people will tell you that it's primarily your interview, negotiation skills and salary history that determine your salary offer. Those are all important factors, but you'll want to prime the salary pump by presenting yourself as the perfect candidate in your resume. In fact, the info you present in writing can be so finely tuned to a job offer that employers may just boost their initial salary offers in response. Here are some tips from hiring professionals on how to make that happen.

If you want to maximize the dollar signs potential employers see when they look at your resume, you've got to make your summary statement so enticing that they will covet your skills for their firms, says Dr. Marlene Caroselli, a corporate trainer and author of dozens of management books. Caroselli offers examples of two summary statements that fail in this effort and one that succeeds:

- Poor example: "Curriculum writer with many years' experience in a wide variety of employment situations."

The example lacks specificity and hence fails to grab a reader's attention, she says. "Curriculum writer" is a vague term that could apply to a second-grade teacher or a corporate trainer. "Many years" is equally vague, Caroselli continues; it could mean three years or 20 years. "Wide variety" could mean the same teacher taught both second and third grades.

- Poor example: "World-recognized author of instructional design materials with a client base of Fortune 100 companies and Department of Defense."

This example sounds "self-serving and possibly untrue," Caroselli says. "There really aren't many people" who can claim to be "world-recognized" authors, she notes. It's also needlessly limited. "If the applicant has worked for more than one agency in the federal government, why limit the statement to just DoD?"

- Good example: "Instructional designer with 20 years experience providing training products and services to Fortune 100 companies and the federal government. Recognized name in HR publishing field, with worldwide clients."

This summary statement is more specific, citing a precise number of years experience as well as impressive client citations: "Fortune 100 companies and the federal government. The well-written summary will do two things: intimate the

> Sensitive employee data can be be inadvertantly leaked. One survey reported that 62 percent of companies had experienced such a security breach in one year.

CHANGE YOUR RESUME, CHANGE YOUR LIFE

 Only rarely will a job seeker admit to having left one job simply to go to a new city where no job is waiting but a happier life may be. That is, you don't hear it often from anyone who has outgrown their 20s, let alone their 30s or 40s.

Jill G., 50-something, did just that, and ended up in a new environment and a new job she loves. "My husband and I lived in the Midwest our whole lives, and we'd reached a point where we were both disenchanted with our jobs," says Jill, who worked as a marketing manager in Des Moines, Iowa, for a series of advertising agencies and veterinary pharmaceutical companies. "We decided that if we were both going to look for new jobs, why do it in Des Moines? We just said, 'We're done with the cold and the snow' and moved to Texas."

Jill and her husband, a CPA, packed up the car and drove south, ending up between San Antonio and Austin, where they looked around to see if they liked the place. They decided they did, rented a house, then drove back north to pick up the rest of their stuff.

"We have no kids; all our family is back in Indiana, so we had nothing holding us back," Jill says. "We did a lot of planning financially, so we knew how long we could last. If neither of us had another job by July, we would re-evaluate; if neither of us had anything by October, we'd move back to Iowa, where we still had a house." It didn't take that long, although the insecurity of not having a job and shock of having to find one in a place where she was completely unknown made Jill's three months of unemployment more stressful than she'd expected.

MARKETING YOURSELF

She hadn't had to look for a job among strangers since getting into the marketing business after college. "For 20-something years, my job moves were due to somebody recruiting me based on my experience; they knew me or my work," she recounts. "For that first interview [in Texas], I was very ill-prepared. I thought it would be just like before—it would be fine. They didn't know who I was and could have cared less. Looking back on my resume and performance, they must have thought I was some kind of idiot."

Jill spent days researching best-practices articles on how to do a job interview, how to write a resume and how to search for jobs online. She realized she had spent years helping companies market products but never thought about how to market herself.

A resume evaluation from TheLadders helped turn that corner. "The woman who evaluated my resume implied it was a wonder I got any calls," Jill says. Her resume listed her jobs and education but didn't put the highlights of her career up front or emphasize her most visible strengths and accomplishments. It also didn't create a recognizable person or set of skills that would catch the eye of a recruiter or hiring manager faced with dozens or hundreds of resumes.

"I sat down and really rewrote it and took a really hard, honest look at myself," Jill says. "I had to dig back and look at my accomplishments over time. A lot of things I had done I hadn't thought that much about at the time, so I hadn't written anything down. I had to go back and remember all that and describe it and why it was important. It was a real shock."

Her resume consultant identified specific accomplishments to highlight—not just that Jill had helped launch a product, but that it was a USDA-regulated product the company was able to ship in an unusually quick 18 months, and that after X number of months on the market the product garnered Y amount of sales.

"IF I CAN SELL A TOOTHBRUSH FOR A CAT ..."

"It was all about specific ways

you helped a company move forward," Jill says. "And in the interview, too, you have to walk in and tell them exactly what you can do for them and tell about a time in the past that you did that for someone else. I told them how once I had worked for a company that, among other things, made toothpaste and toothbrushes for dogs and cats. I said, 'If I can sell a toothbrush for a cat, I can sell anything.' "

As it turned out, being able to sell things for animals—if not dogs and cats—was the key to landing a new job in marketing at a company that makes products designed to sequence and analyze DNA and RNA samples, often for companies diagnosing sick animals or making drugs or other health-related products for them.

"[The company] posted this job that said they needed someone with an animal-science degree who had done marketing with animal products," Jill says. "I pulled it off and said, 'This is who I am.'"

GOING BACK TO HER ROOTS

Jill graduated college with a degree in animal science, which covers most of the health and biochemistry issues that affect agribusiness: diseases and medicines for cattle and chickens, animal biochemistry, and other topics critical to those running commercial farms and ranches.

She spent her career in Iowa working mostly for companies marketing products and pharmaceuticals to animals—usually farm animals rather than dogs and cats. So when the company needed marketing help for a small division in Austin selling products designed for veterinary diagnostic labs trying to identify avian flu or salmonella in farm animals, the match seemed perfect.

HAPPY ENDING

"The recruiter told me, and this is the first time I ever heard this, that they weren't even talking to any other candidates because they didn't expect to find me," Jill says. "You want to be humble, but in this situation, you just can't. You have to find the one or two things you can do for them," she says.

"I asked them to give me a specific challenge they had, the hardest thing they're facing. Based on that, I could say, 'Here's something I did in the past to solve a similar problem and what I would do to solve this one.' It's almost like consulting advice; you run the risk of being way off-base, but even if you are, they like that you have opinions."

Another trick that worked well was to remember the kinds of books on the shelf of the hiring managers who had interviewed her. At the new company, one manager had a marketing-theory book called *"Blue Ocean Strategy: How to Create Uncontested Market Space and Make Competition Irrelevant"* by W. Chan Kim and Renée Mauborgne.

"I went out and bought a copy and skimmed it," she says. "So in my follow-up note I was able to say I thought they needed to pursue a Blue Ocean strategy to differentiate themselves and made some suggestions on how to do it."

It worked. She got the job and has been in love with it ever since. Texas worked out, too. Jill's husband put off finding full-time work to act as general contractor on a house the two are building.

It's 75 degrees and sunny in Austin. "I have yet to put on a jacket this year," Jill says. "I just love it."

real value of the applicant, and prompt the employer to offer as much as he or she can so this prospect won't go elsewhere," Caroselli says.

Don't Go Overboard

A WORD OF CAUTION about maximizing your potential salary offers: There's pumping up your worth, and then there's just plain old puffery. While it's certainly important to put the best possible spin on your jobs and accomplishments, it's just as important not to go too far, says Shel Horowitz, a marketing consultant who dubs himself the "Ethical Marketing Expert."

Horowitz recalled a librarian who approached him with a resume written by a professional resume writer that exaggerated so much that the woman was uncomfortable. Her resume "had described a library page job as if it was a library director" position, he says. "It had gone so far over the line that there was zero credibility."

Horowitz toned down the job description but also took care to delineate the progression of skills his client acquired as she continued her career. The woman was hired shortly after as a library department director. "Honestly, I don't think she would have been offered the position had she pretended to have had directorial responsibilities as a page," he says.

The bottom line on maximizing salary potential with your resume is this: You can come off as pure gold in your resume, but if you can't support that impression in the interview, your chances of a job offer shrink. "Sometimes I have contacted people who have great resumes" but who act unprofessionally in an interview and whose subsequent e-mails contain grammar and spelling errors, he says. "You interview them, and they're not a grand thing at all." Your resume is your chance to get your foot in the door. Make sure the rest of you matches the foot.

CHECKLIST: RESUME

Follow these best practices to ensure your resume isn't screened out by an applicant tracking system or HR manager.

○ **Do not apply to a company multiple times** if the positions do not match your experience and skills. Recruiters notice multiple submissions, and it reflects poorly on a candidate if he applies for jobs that aren't a good fit.

○ **But if you're being referred by an employee,** make sure the ATS knows it; the software's smart enough to care.

○ **Don't send your resume as an attachment.** To avoid getting caught by security scans, paste it into the body of the e-mail.

○ **Include a professional or executive summary at the resume top,** followed by a list of bulleted qualifications and/or achievements.

○ **Customize the professional/executive summary** and bulleted list(s) with keywords that match a given job.

○ **Make sure the keywords** in the executive summary and bulleted qualifications and achievements replicate those in the job posting.

○ **If the ATS offers options,** choose to upload your resume instead of cutting and pasting. This feature often parses information and saves it in the optimal format, ensuring the cleanest presentation.

○ **To avoid "choking" an ATS with a highly formatted resume,** make sure yours is in a clear, concise format, with your contact information located at the top instead of in the header or footer.

○ **Do not include graphics on a resume;** they can garble the information the ATS processes.

○ **When reapplying after an initial rejection,** tweak executive summaries and bulleted lists of key skills and achievements; never adjust the elements of your work history.

○ **When reapplying,** avoid creating a duplicate record in the system by using a different e-mail address than the one you used on your first try. This isn't enough to avoid a duplicate record in advanced systems.

○ **Once your customized resume has been resubmitted,** contact the appropriate recruiter (or sympathetic administrative assistant) and request that your updated resume be reviewed for the open position.

PERS

DRESSING TO INTERVIEW
ON THE SLY

LUNCH WITH A CONNECTED FRIEND

AN IMAGI MAKEOVER— A NEW SHO AT SUCCES

LOSE THE FRUMP FA

BRAN

ONAL

BEHIND THE REWRITE: BUILDING A WINNING
RESUME

WEEP
OUR
VEB
RAIL | ## DRESS TO NETWORK—EVERY ENCOUNTER COUNTS

TOR, WIN THE JOB

DING

"Building your personal brand" might strike you as a funny way of thinking about your career, but the idea has been around for centuries.

The ancient Greeks called it *arete*, and it meant being the best you can be. During the time of knights and castles, it was called "honor," and you were expected to defend it to the death. George Washington and men of his era were extremely concerned about maintaining and protecting their reputation. And in the 20th century, it might have been referred to as your standing in your community or your industry.

So "personal brand" is simply a new phrase for an old concept—how you present yourself to others.

You know all the wonderful experiences you've had, and you're intimately familiar with all the capabilities you've developed through your career. That's always been an integral part of personal success. But your success is as dependent on what others think about what you can do as it is on what you can actually do.

The big change in modern times is scale.

The Greeks had only to be concerned with people living in their city; knights with their honor within the kingdom; Washington with his reputation within the colonies; and in the 20th century, your standing was dependent on your community and your industry.

What's changed is the modern economy. Companies can

vaporize overnight. Whole industries can be upended by a change in technology, regulation or globalization.

So what's important now is that your brand be known and available not only to the people of your city, state, country or industry, but to any professional at any time. You never know when you'll be tossed into a new industry, a new city or a new company, so it's important for you to consider how you'll be perceived and how your background and skills will be interpreted by others.

Adding to the tumultuousness of the modern economy, modern technology has bestowed upon us Google, social networks, blogs and a host of other means for others to learn about your "*arete*," your honor, your reputation, your standing, in ways other than speaking directly with you.

In that sense, then, building your personal brand is about understanding how you want your professional life to be seen by others, and then managing your presence towards that end. So while it's a new phrase, it's an old concept, and in this chapter we'll address everything from Google to good-looking shoes.

An Image Makeover—A New Shot at Success

SOMETIMES IT TAKES MORE than just a little self-knowledge and chutzpah to get what you want. Sometimes it takes someone with an outside perspective to help you see that you may be frustrated in pursuing a goal—not because you can't reach it but because it's not the right one in the first place.

In the case of Laura Warren, the right job turns out not to be the mid-level marketing positions she was pursuing in a $230 billion cosmetics industry dominated by Estee Lauder and L'Oreal, against which she competed as an independent. The right job comes out of charity and community work, a path that feels to her like advocating for important causes and looks to a career counselor like the background and contacts of a successful lobbyist or political operative.

Chasing the wrong job was more a matter of momentum and reluctance to take advantage of friends than it was a conscious career decision. After nine years of fighting for and running her own color-cosmetics business, Warren knew she needed a job, so she went after one in the industry in which she'd most recently worked.

Unfortunately, all her experience in cosmetics was in working for herself, not for companies among whom, she says, a 57-year-old woman isn't the most sought-after commodity.

"Everything is fine in e-mail or on the phone, until I go to the interview," explains Warren of her job search and inability to get past what appeared to be the refusal of industry recruiters or hiring managers to consider a candidate who is older than the one they might have expected.

"If [the interviewer] is someone younger than I am, 38 or 40 maybe, then it's an issue," she says. "If they're younger than that, they just have no time for you. They seem to be following a formula, and if you don't fit, it's hard to talk your way through that barrier. They're not interested in a history of success as much as they are a profile."

But was it really her age that was working against her? Or did the problem lie in the way she was marketing herself—and to whom?

The problem Warren was running into was that she was not only applying for jobs that were too low-level for her skills, she was ignoring her greatest strengths and assets to interview for jobs that weren't half as important as the work she did on a volunteer basis.

"She had a great deal of energy that was wildly diffused," says Josh Klenoff, president of JKCoaching.com. "In our first coaching session I knew my job was to help focus that energy. We took inventory of the elements of her past or skills that would help her to thrive, adapted those to what she might think would be her ideal job, and focused her on how to land that job."

> **Was it really her age that was working against her? Or did the problem lie in the way she was marketing herself—and to whom?**

Friends in High Places

ONE STUMBLING BLOCK was the limited range of contacts with whom Warren was networking. She was talking to recruiters and colleagues in the cosmetics business but had not even approached friends and colleagues she made doing political or business-development or charity work.

Warren is a member of the board of governors of the Los Angeles Economic Development Council, for example, a southern California lobbying and business-development group whose executive committee and board of governors include senior executives from Time Warner, Wachovia, Bank of America, Sony Pictures, as well as some of the largest, most powerful entertainment, transportation, real estate, manufacturing and other businesses in southern California.

LAEDC's reports focus on the performance of California businesses; recommendations for changes on regulatory, business or political issues; and forecasts of economic performance that are often among the earliest hints that big economic changes are about to take place. Warren has been an active member for years, spending tremendous amounts of her own time working on committees, reports and issues she considers important to the business and political climates of southern California.

When industry trade group the Cosmetic, Toiletry and Fragrance Association needed a contact in the California legislature to raise objections to "legislation that was going to be very bad for the cosmetics industry in California," Warren says, they called her. "I was a member of CTFA, but I also knew all these other people. I gave them a name to call, a friend sitting in the legislature, and I called her and said, 'I want you to be nice to these people.' It worked out very well," she remembers.

Though she's the only cosmetics-industry executive on the board, her contacts and experience go far beyond cosmetics. She has deep expertise—and numerous contacts—in the international shipping industry, in entertainment, and at the high end of the art world.

She began her professional career in the shipping business in the Port of Los Angeles—a family tradition in which she was the third generation. She started in office work, helping to establish the first West Coast headquarters of Evergreen Marine Corp., the Chinese shipping company that became a giant of Pacific shipping.

She is still proud of her membership in the International Longshore and Warehouse Union, in which she rose through the docks hierarchy, managing the schedules and paperwork involved in loading the huge ships and eventually heading the maritime claims group responsible for making good when a rogue wave or loose tarp left cargo water-damaged or lost at sea.

"I loved working with the Chinese and people from all over the Far East," Warren says. "I picked up Mandarin after a while. The Chinese are fascinating; they're all about results. We got along very well!"

Where she didn't get along was with the culture of the docks that, even in 1994, made it impossible for a woman to be seriously considered as vessel superinten-dent, the staffer who coordinates the movement of cargo on and off ships. It was the only role in vessel operations missing from her resume, and she didn't like the limitation.

She learned to negotiate in the rough conditions and multiple languages of the maritime industry, in which management and the unions might be at each other's throats over an issue, and sometimes might be unable to understand each other because of language or cultural barriers. After negotiations were settled, though, everyone still had to work together.

"That's where I learned my technique for negotiating, which my friends refer to as 'pouring tea,' " Warren says. "You pour tea and remain calm and polite and just keep talking. It's diplomacy."

She learned how to negotiate more softly with celebrities, wealthy benefactors and art collectors, after shifting into the high-end art world to support her then-husband, a well-regarded painter of the Taos School. She took a relatively low-level job at the Biltmore Galleries, a top-end art gallery, but was quickly promoted to executive director, the No. 2 position.

The job required discretion—celebrities and wealthy clients don't like to be gos-siped about—a rich understanding of art in a rapidly changing market, and extraor-dinary tact to deal with both clients and artists of unpredictable mien. "I handled all the live artists because the owners loved the dead ones. They loved them because they were dead," Warren says.

Though she doesn't talk about them without pressure and doesn't name them at all, the people she works with on charity projects, economic-development projects and groups like the LAEDC make up a contact network that covers most of the rich and powerful in southern California.

"I never looked at my network for myself," Warren says, with a bit of bewilderment, a day after her conference with Klenoff. "I always looked at it for trade academies, for the Port of Los Angeles, problems with the community. I don't hesitate to advocate if the issue makes sense. But I never really looked at it for myself."

From Beggar to Marketer

WARREN'S ISSUE IS ONE OF PERCEPTION. Even accomplished people feel as if they're going hat in hand when they ask powerful, wealthy or well-connected friends for help.

"They'll say, 'I feel like I'm asking for favors,' " Klenoff explains. "It's a beggar mindset. That's not a powerful place to be coming from. The alternative is a mar-

BEHIND THE REWRITE: BUILDING A WINNING RESUME

Professional resume writers don't usually take it as a positive sign when they ask a new client for a copy of an existing resume and are told, " I just deleted it."

It might suggest the client is a little careless with what's supposed to be a thumbnail history of his or her own. Or it might reflect a lot of determination to change course.

In the case of Laura Warren, it appears to have been the latter. Warren was unhappily pursuing mid- to senior-level executive positions in the cosmetics industry until a session with a career coach helped her realize that politics, public activism and the life of a professional lobbyist fit the reality of her life much better than a marketing gig at L'Oreal.

According to Becky T., the resume writer at TheLadders who worked with Warren, this career switcher had a hard time promoting her real strengths and accomplishments.

TURN YOUR RESUME UPSIDE DOWN

"With most resumes you focus on not just the companies people work for but what they did for them," Becky explains. "With Laura, it was the other stuff that mattered to presenting her effectively as a lobbyist, without any formal lobbying experience."

So, rather than a resume that starts with one paragraph on the job seeker's goals and another on her skills and accomplishments at past jobs, Warren's new resume showcases her experience and contributions running her own company and at other organizations. It shows her immediate value as a lobbyist, talking about her experience in contacts at places she worked, even though they weren't part of a formal job description. "Her work with these organizations and the people she knows and what she accomplished are what she's trying to leverage as experience as a lobbyist, so that's the focus of the resume," says Becky.

keting mindset. You see yourself as a product, and you can see that anyone who can get that product to the customer who values it—the employer—will also get a value out of it."

After realizing the untapped power of her network, Klenoff and Warren reviewed her other strengths and decided that her ability to collar politicians, friends and business contacts to talk about issues she thought were important were more than just a personal strength.

"We talked about lobbying as a career, and it's just a natural fit," Warren says. "I'm a natural-born advocate if something makes sense to me. I have a very sound background in maritime—not only ocean but air and rail—as well as entertainment and cosmetics and other international business.

"Maritime transport and entertainment are very hard-pressed in this state. Growth, taxes, business-unfriendly environments and other states that are enticing businesses away from California—we're competing with other states for port development," remarks Warren, listing a few of her hot-button issues. "I understand business, and I'm used to working with politicians; I know how they work."

"This change in perspective put her on a completely different playing field,"

Klenoff says of this turning point. "When we first talked, she was unclear on her next steps. It's not at all uncommon, and people can spend a year in that place." Soon, however, "She had a path and it's one in which she can use her wellspring of resources, her knowledge, her intuition. So creating a new metaphor for herself was helpful. It was a quantum leap in progress for her."

It took Warren only one phone call to get started on the new course. She phoned a close friend and contact who is active in southern California business and politics, and whose husband is a player in judicial circles.

"They understood immediately that I was talking about myself," she notes. "She said, 'Yes, darling. Come over Sunday and we'll talk, we'll make sure some doors open for you.' They're thrilled I came to this realization because they know I can do it. I just didn't know it was OK to ask. I'm amazed."

Lose the "Frump Factor," Win the Job

YOU MAY SPEND HOURS revamping your resume, researching the company and practicing your selling points. But if your outward appearance does not reflect your energy and enthusiasm about the position, chances are someone else's will. In a perfect world, we would all be judged on our inner beauty and the most qualified candidate would always get the gig. Unfortunately, style, charisma, connections and the proverbial cool factor all play an influential role when considering job candidates.

If you haven't thought about these things in a while, chances are your go-to-interview look could use an update. You don't want to dress too young for your age, but who doesn't want to appear 10 years younger? The right outfit can increase your confidence and make a lasting first impression.

The word "fashion" can be intimidating, but what you are really trying to do is update your personal style, not look like a runway model. If you like classic cuts and play-it-safe solids, then stick to what you are comfortable with; the most important thing is to focus on finding a modern cut and a flawless fit. Have a penchant for flair? Try wearing interesting shapes and statement accessories.

Below are a few simple rules to ensure that whatever your personal style, your professional look is modern and memorable (in the good way!):

Clothes have an expiration date.
Secretary blouses, pleated pants, mid-calf anything—if these items are in your work wardrobe, chances are they weren't a recent purchase. Unless it is a custom-made Armani suit, several years' wear and tear alone are reason enough to lay clothes to rest. Take this chance to rid your professional wardrobe of anything more than five

years old, except for a couple of investment pieces that were made to last you a life-time. This will ensure that you are rid of dated shapes and any fabrics that might not appear fresh.

Fit is a factor.

If it is too tight or too big, you will not only feel uncomfortable but look it as well. Common problem areas are snug jacket arms that pull across the back, blouses that ripple across the chest, and pants that are too tight in the middle or sag in the seat. Lose those pieces you hope to fit back into one day and the baggier ones that you have been "meaning" to take to the tailor. When shopping for replacement items, it is normal for most women to fall in between sizes. Rule of thumb: Size up and find an impeccable tailor to fit it to your body.

Fashion Tips for Women

Choose shapes that flatter your body.

This tip seems obvious, but unfortunately we have been programmed to reach for certain silhouettes when it comes to dressing for a formal interview—pencil skirt and button-down, check. The truth is these two cuts don't look great on most women. Pencil skirts are unforgiving if you have even the slightest of hips, and button-downs are notorious for bulging open in all the wrong places. Instead, if you are curvy, opt for A-line skirts and dresses that provide a slimming effect on the lower body and scoop-necked shells that lay smooth under jackets. If you are petite, try a fitted sheath that falls just above the knee, which is both professional and attractive.

Hose are a thing of the past.

Yes, you can start celebrating: Hosiery, at least any that is visible, are no longer a requirement for women in the workplace. They should be avoided altogether, except for women who want to smooth their legs. In that case, they should be very sheer and match your natural skin color. (No tan, please!) On the other hand, opaque tights are acceptable and encouraged during the winter months, when boots are the only suitable shoe option. They also look chic when worn with patent-leather pumps. But unless you want to look like Rainbow Brite, stick to black tights, even when wearing neutral colors.

Shoes and bags are your style outlet.

It is a myth that an interview requires a basic black shoe and masculine briefcase. In fact, when keeping your clothes simple and chic, your shoes and bag are a great way to add sophistication and style. Have fun with oxford-inspired booties, patent-leather pumps, peep-toed Mary Janes and tastefully colored totes and animal-skin satchels (faux if you prefer!). The only rules are no white shoes and no strappy sandals, ever.

Wear a dress.

While a skirt or pantsuit is always appropriate, so is a great dress and jacket. From simple sheaths to A-line styles, a dress is the most flattering silhouette a woman can wear. Stick to solid wovens, tweeds and delicate pinstripes. If you are more fashion-forward, try a cocoon shape, a '60s shift or a '50s-style dress with a fuller skirt and wide belt. Bonus: A dress takes the guesswork out of the what-blouse-to-wear dilemma.

Wear navy, black and gray—together.

Navy, black and gray should be the three staple colors of your professional wardrobe, with a few brightly colored accent pieces. These colors look great with everything and even better when worn together. Try a black tweed suit with a navy silk blouse for a sophisticated look. Wear a black fitted blazer with a navy shift dress and black patent belt for a fashion statement. Try a charcoal-gray chiffon dress with a navy cropped jacket if you prefer ultra-feminine pieces.

Add some flair.

The right belt or earrings can make your otherwise boring and predictable outfit impressive and memorable. Wear a wide belt in patent leather or a skinny gold belt to accentuate your waist. Try delicate gold hoops instead of stuffy pearls to modernize your basic jewelry. Wear a necklace in gray beads or any soft color to highlight your neckline and create an air of sophistication.

Experiment with fabrics.

Rayon and polyester are not executive-worthy textiles. Fill your closet with light-weight tweeds, linen blends, silk blends and even bouclé. Texture in a suit or dress can add a personal touch and keeps your look seasonal. In the winter opt for a tweed jacket over a black wool sheath, black opaque tights and patent-leather sling-backs. In the summer, a linen pencil skirt, crisp white blouse. and neutral pointed-toe pumps look elegant and fresh.

Purchase a versatile basic.

There is no need to purchase a whole wardrobe just to update your look. The key is working with a couple of investment pieces to create a versatile, modern look. Splurge on a black sheath that flatters your body type, a navy A-line skirt and a black tailored jacket with slimming bracelet sleeves. The black sheath will work with the jacket, alone with a statement belt, or with a crisp button-down or soft blouse layered underneath. The navy skirt can be paired with a printed blouse and jacket, a crisp white shirt or a camisole and belted cardigan. Shop for solid basics in flattering silhouettes and make them work for you. In other words—wear them all the time!

Fashion Tips for Men

Pleated pants add bulge.
If you think your pleated-front pants are disguising your spare tire, you are unfortunately mistaken. The excess fabric is only adding bulk to your midsection and causing you to look heavier than you are. Opt for a flat-front suit pant, and voila: ten pounds thinner.

Put your best shirt forward.
Your dress shirt is not a place to get creative. Save your style statement for a sharp-looking tie and a sophisticated watch. Avoid white contrast-collar shirts; gingham prints, fussy cufflinks, and, most importantly, short sleeves. Dress shirts in solids or small stripes in white, blue, ecru and gray are the most versatile investments.

Wear a power tie.
This term is not limited to solid red. Look for ties in blues, yellows, black and mauve, as they are the most versatile. Don't be afraid of a small design or wide stripe; just make sure it is easy on the eyes and not political.

Give them a try—slim-fit suits.
"Slim fit" is a phrase that has been misconstrued. All that a slim-fit style suit refers to is streamlined tailoring. They cut the bulky (sometimes saggy) fabric out of the upper leg and the middle of a coat, and the lapels tend to be narrower. This causes the suit pants to hang more nicely through the leg, and you avoid a boxy-cut coat. Slim-fit suits are not just for the younger crowd, either; all the major suiting retailers are designing slim styles.

Love your tailor.
And listen to his advice. He has seen more than his fair share of suits in his day, so take heed. Fit is the most important factor when it comes to a suit. An expensive suit that doesn't fit might as well be from the Goodwill bin. The same goes for a less expensive suit; if exquisitely tailored, no one will be the wiser.

Your shoes, belt and briefcase matter.

These key accessories should not be the oldest things in your closet. For an updated briefcase, opt for an over-the-shoulder messenger-style in a rich leather. Wingtips are the sharp go-to shoes; for a more relaxed look, try a penny loafer. Wear a belt with detail, whether in classic black or with a structured buckle. Your shoes, belt and briefcase don't all have to be cut from the same leather; choose leathers that complement one another but have a slight variation in colors to avoid looking too "matchy-matchy."

You look better in navy.

It is natural to lean toward investing in a black suit, but navy is proven to be a more universally flattering color. A dark-blue suit in a solid or delicate pinstripe is less harsh on most skin tones. Hate navy? Your second-best choice is charcoal.

Two-button coats slim you.

Trade your classic three-button for a leaner looking two-button suit coat. They make you look trimmer through the stomach compared to the three-button style, which can cause rumples and rolls when buttoned.

Wear complementary colors.

Your suit, dress shirt and tie must all be in a palette of colors that work with one another. A navy suit worn with a gray shirt and yellow tie is not complementary. Here are some palettes to refer to when choosing your interview attire:
  • Gray, steel blue, mauve and white
  • Black, red, yellow, white and powder blue
  • Navy, French blue, lavender and ecru

Pay attention to details.

Avoid argyle socks and political tie clips. Tie clips should be solid metal with small design details, while socks are best in solid colors such as blue or black solids. Pocket squares in classic white are also a nice touch for a formal look, if that's a look you can pull off.

Dressing to Interview on the Sly

IN A CORPORATE CULTURE where business casual is making waves, showing up to work in a three-piece suit is a dead giveaway to your colleagues that your dentist appointment is really an interview—somewhere else. Fortunately, there are a few simple ways to tone down your look for the office but avoid a fashion overhaul in the cramped restroom before your interview. By pairing a few casual items with your more formal interview attire, it will be anybody's guess why you look just a little more polished today.

Women

1. Wear flat boots or ballet flats.

Leave your gorgeous pumps under your desk in favor of lower heels. Bare legs and ballet flats or riding boots with tights will instantly dress down your interview-appropriate skirt. Bonus: Your feet will thank you.

2. Trade your jacket for a soft cardigan.

Layer a cozy cardigan in a soft color over your interview blouse or dress. Cardigans evoke a sense of casualness not usually appropriate for a formal interview. Leave your jacket hanging in your car or at your desk. Bonus: It will stay wrinkle-free.

3. Add a fashionable scarf or trendy jewelry.

A boldly colored necklace or Pucci printed scarf are a bit too fashion-forward for a formal interview. However, fun accessories can be added to your interview attire for a whimsical look; just don't forget to tone them down before your meeting. Bonus: Compliments from your colleagues.

Men

1. Leave off your jacket and tie.

In this case, it is all about what you don't wear. If a formal suit isn't in your office dress code, simply leave your jacket and tie off till the interview. Bonus: Comfort! Isn't that enough?

2. Wear a sport coat or pullover sweater.

If you prefer to wear a coat to the office, opt for a more casual sport coat or a cozy pullover. These layers will instantly dress down your suit pants and button-down. Bonus: Style points for mixing it up.

3. Keep your shoes casual.

Leave your shiny Allen Edmonds under your desk in favor of a casual loafer or driving shoe. A low-key shoe even when worn with suit pants will clearly deter your colleagues from suspecting that you are looking for work elsewhere. Bonus: Your shoeshine will stay fresh.

MUST HAVES

Five things every man needs
- An unlined wool suit jacket
- A handkerchief
- Breath strips
- A shoeshine
- A proper, structured leather briefcase with handles

Five things every woman needs
- A medium-size canvas or leather tote bag
- A statement necklace
- Ballet flats
- Frizz-reducing hair product
- A structured, sleeveless, belted dress

DRESS TO NETWORK—EVERY ENCOUNTER COUNTS

Got a lunch date with a friend who knows a friend who has a friend who is hiring? Did the boss invite you to join him at the Yankees game? Schmoozing at a gallery opening? If your calendar is chock-full of potential networking opportunities, it's time to make an appointment with your closet as well.

A JOB FAIR

Attending a job fair is like speed dating. You should be dressed for the possibility of an in-the-moment interview. In other words, wear a suit.

Women: A dress is appropriate as well, when paired with a tailored jacket. Stick to a flattering palette of black, navy, gray or cream. Keep jewelry delicate, but carry a chic tote. (It's not fashionable to schlep a canvas bag full of resumes!)

Men: You know the rules: well fitting suit, power tie and polished shoes.

LUNCH WITH A CONNECTED FRIEND

Your old college buddy wants to do lunch and might be bringing a big-time player in your industry along. A business associate wants to get your thoughts over lunch on a new venture he's considering. Whatever the circumstance, lunch can be a tricky style situation. You want to be dressed to impress, but too formal sends the impression that you are too eager and don't respect the social aspect of the meeting. Rule of thumb: Wear business casual with an emphasis on the casual.

Women: Wear your favorite separates, like a slim skirt and printed blouse. Avoid looking stuffy by ditching your jacket, closed-toed shoes and oversized work tote. Opt for pretty heels and a smaller handbag—no resume required!

Men: Keep your look casual in dark jeans or crisp khakis and a button-down in a classic color. Wear your suit jacket on top to add the right element of professionalism. No tie required, but a leather belt with a square metal buckle and sleek oxfords will complete your look.

A COCKTAIL PARTY

A great debate in the fashion arena is what defines "cocktail attire." Short dress? Suit and tie required? While these are up for discussion, remember one thing: It is always better to be overdressed than underdressed.

Women: Choose a cocktail dress that is flattering and exposes a tasteful amount of skin. No plunging necklines or bandage dresses, please. Look for a hem that grazes the knee—any longer and you will look dated; any shorter and you will look like you belong in a club. Dresses made in chiffon or silk lie nicer than satin, which tends to rumple in all the wrong places. A silhouette that flatters almost any women's body is sleeveless with a scoop neck, fitted waist and slightly fuller skirt. Stick to colors that translate well at night: black, gray, shades of red and navy. Wear open-toed heels and your favorite ear or neck sparklers for a finishing touch.

Men: You need to wear a suit. Your best suit. Use this opportunity to experiment with colors. In other words, save your black suit for the office. Try suits in shades of gray or tan. Tiny-printed or solid-color ties give a dressier appearance appropriate for a cocktail party. Add a tiny pocket square for a finishing touch.

DRINKS WITH A COLLEAGUE

Grabbing a cocktail with a co-worker? Meeting a potential employer for a Scotch? Your daytime look will require some minor adjustments for the bar.

Women: Wear a blouse or dress with tasteful embellishments, whether it has sheen, a beaded design or simply a row of ruffles. This will allow your look to translate easily from day to night. Ditch unwanted layers such as tights, jackets or cardigans. Last, add a fashionable necklace in colorful jewels, and don't forget to switch your day tote for a sleek clutch. Transformation complete!

Men: Lose your jacket, roll up your sleeves and slightly loosen your tie for a relaxed look. Add a fashionable vest or casual sport coat for a style statement.

A CONFERENCE OR SEMINAR

A gathering of industry professionals or a business seminar is a great way to network with new people. With an opportunity to zero in on specific industry influencers, it is key you make a good first impression. While formal attire is not required, you don't want to be caught shaking hands without a jacket on your arm. Your look for these opportunities should be business casual, with an emphasis on business.

Women: Sick of your skirt-and-blouse office routine? Use this opportunity to wear a flattering

shift dress in a rich color. With a hem right around the knee and a minimal neckline, this is the perfect notice-me look. Closed-toed heels and a sleek tote will ensure you look professional.

Men: See "A job fair." (Only you don't need to be wearing your jacket; it's there for security, just in case.)

TICKETS TO THE BIG GAME

What to wear when drinking beer and eating nachos with the boss while watching his favorite sports team? In such a casual environment, dressing with a business purpose in mind is tricky. The key to looking relaxed yet professional is choosing the right fabrics and showing the appropriate amount of skin. As a rule, the attire should be weekend casual.

Women: Although you might usually grab a tank top and shorts for game day, when networking, opt for a little less skin. Try cotton shorts with at least a 5-inch inseam, and tuck in an airy button-down in linen or chambray. Wear flat sandals, no flip-flops. Classic aviators and a sporty watch will easily complete your look.

Men: Reach for your weekend pants, like lightweight chinos or classic jeans, but avoid sporting

shorts. A cotton polo will keep you cool, but the collar will keep you looking cleaned up. Wear sandals or sleek sneakers. However, no flip-flops. But feel free to wear your favorite baseball hat!

WEEKEND BARBECUE

Whether headed to a Fourth of July blowout or a more intimate birthday celebration for a colleague, barbecues are a great chance to meet friends of friends and expand your professional network. But unless you are manning the grill, your look needs to send the right message. No crop- or tank tops allowed!

Women: Try a breezy denim skirt (stay away from minis) and striped knit tank. Make sure that the straps are thick enough that you won't have any bra-strap mishaps. Metallic sandals and a chunky bracelet add just the right amount of polish. A knee-length sundress (avoid halters) is also a stylish choice.

Men: Khaki or navy shorts (no jean shorts, ever!) are a temperature-friendly option for barbecues. Try a polo shirt in a classic color, as T-shirts tend to look sloppy. Avoid wearing a hat so you can make good eye contact. Lastly, brown leather sandals are more sophisticted than flip-flops.

101

CHECKLIST: SWEEP YOUR WEB TRAIL

Follow these steps to review your online profile and make sure it is spotless before recruiters and potential employers see it. If you use any of the major social networks, start your Web cleanup there.

LINKEDIN

○ **1. Updated:** Check for accurate and updated information.

○ **2. Keywords:** Insert keywords that will be important to the new job you seek. Make sure they are presented prominently and frequently.

○ **3. "Contact Me":** Check the "Contact Me" option. Many recruiters search LinkedIn only for candidates willing to be contacted.

FACEBOOK

○ **1. Updated:** Check for accurate and updated information. Complete your work history.

○ **2. Keywords:** Insert keywords that will be important to the new job you seek.

○ **3. Search:** Go to the "Privacy Settings" section. If you want to be found by recruiters on Facebook and are comfortable with what they will find, set search visibility to "Everyone on Facebook." If you want to reserve Facebook for your personal life, limit it accordingly.

○ **4. Public Search:** Also in the privacy settings, check "Public Search Listing," which will allow anyone outside of Facebook to locate you with other search engines.

○ **5. Friend Lists:** Set separate networks for private and professional contacts. Add new contacts to the appropriate network.

○ **6. Photos:** On the Privacy Settings page, change the "Photos Tagged of You" setting to "Only Me" and "None of my Networks."

○ **7. Facebook Applications:** Check to see which applications are visible on your profile page and alter settings to limit who sees what.

○ **8. Wall Posts:** Alter privacy settings to limit who can write on your Facbook Wall and who can read posts to your Wall.

JOB BOARDS

○ **1. Updated:** Check TheLadders or any other job boards that feature your resume to ensure information is current. Outdated information can be harmful, and possibly confusing to a potential employer.

○ **2. Keywords:** Insert keywords that will be important to the new job you seek.

○ **3. Contacts:** Enable search and "Contact Me" features. Many sites offer features to remain confidential. Ensure they are set to display and search only the information you want public.

GOOGLE

○ **1. Google Search:** Search your own name on Google. This is something a potential employer will do, and it's a good idea to check to see what they will see.
> a. Don't settle for the first 10 results. Check multiple pages.
> b. Search your name + past employers, partners, and so on.
> c. Check the referring pages themselves for inaccurate or embarrassing information.

○ **2. Google Alerts:** Establish Google Alerts for your name and any of the terms you would check in Step 1. As Google finds new information with those terms posted on the Web, you will receive an e-mail or RSS feed.

PHOTOS AND VIDEO

○ **1. Flickr:** This site is open and searchable. Search friends' pictures and "tags" of your name to find pictures of yourself. You must contact the owner of the photo to remove a "tag" or delete a photo.

○ **2. YouTube:** Google's video-storage and social-network Web site is similarly open and will appear in search engine results. Search friends' pictures, videos and "tags" of your name to find footage of yourself. As with Flickr, you must contact the owner of the photo to remove a "tag" or delete a photo.

○ **3. Additional photo and video sites:** There are many other sites such as Facebook, Kodak Gallery, Snapfish, MySpace, Photobucket and Yahoo!Video. Review Google search results.

BLOGS

○ **1. Industry Blogs:** Check these for references to you.

○ **2. Google Blog Search:** Google Blog Search will search sites it identifies as blogs.

○ **3. Clean up:** You can ask a blogger to remove unfavorable information, but if they are uncooperative, be prepared to defend yourself.

TWITTER

○ **1. This social-network technology** can spread word about you quickly, for better or worse. Stay ahead of the curve. Twitter Search your own name to see what people are saying about you.

CLEAN UP

If you've found unfavorable information on the Web about yourself:

○ **1. Fix it:** If you have the ability to edit the Web site, do so.

○ **2. Ask:** Contact that former employer to correct the "About Us" page that still lists you or that friend who's posted embarrassing photos of you.

○ **3. Defend:** If you can't edit or delete, be prepared to defend it in an interview. This is especially true of negative stories in the press, which can be corrected if proven inaccurate but will rarely be removed.

Must-Dos for Your Personal Brand

WHY IT MATTERS: Your career is the most important product you'll ever sell. That means your personal brand has to be polished in every respect, from your documents to your talking points to your personal appearance.

There's a set of written material that must sell your value to any company that hires you, including your resume, cover letter, and collateral such as references and samples. Furthermore, personal branding in the 21st century requires up-to-date online profiles and a real understanding of what recruiters will find when they search for you online.

There's no Web substitute for personal presence and old-fashioned charisma. An effective elevator pitch that quickly describes how you can help your audience succeed — and a personal appearance that's appropriate to your seniority and the situation — are vital to your all-around package.

○ **Resume:** Do you have a professionally written resume that's updated to cover your most recent work experience and capped at 15 years?

○ **Cover letter:** Do you have a short, effective cover letter that can be customized to demonstrate the value you bring to multiple opportunities?

○ **Online presence:** Are your online profiles up-to-date on social networks? Have you searched yourself online to ensure you're prepared for any questions about your public record?

○ **Elevator pitch:** Can you explain smoothly in 30 seconds your intrinsic value to an employer?

○ **References:** Have you identified at least three highly reputable people who've worked with you, including former peers and supervisors? Have you asked them specifically for their permission to act as a reference? Have you gotten their latest contact information? Have you briefed them on what you've done since they last worked with you?

○ **Wardrobe and grooming:** Honestly, do your interview clothes fit you? Are they current and in good shape? Do you head out every day dressed and groomed well enough for an unexpected networking opportunity?

PERSONAL BRANDING OPPORTUNITIES

Document the opportunities to build your personal brand and stake a claim as an expert a

Opportunity	Type of Opportunity (Public speaking, public relations, social media, networking meeting)
Sample: Chamber of Conference Luncheon	Public speaking

your field.

Date Submitted	Date Followed Up	Results
September 9, 2010	September 13, 2010	Delivered speech on trends in SMB software sales to 50+ local CEOs.

GETTING THE JOB WHE

FIVE STEPS TO VOLUNTEE YOUR WAY TO A JO

DON'T IGNORE THE REAL WORLD

NE

WOR

PROMOTE YOUR AMBITION EXPAND YOUR NETWOR

JOB-HUNTING SKILL

YOU'RE OVERQUALIFIED

DON'T IGNORE THE WEB

SOCIAL NETWORK ETIQUETTE

MIND YOUR MANNERS

T-

DON'T BE A CREEP

GET GOOGLED, GET FOUND

PICK YOUR PARTY

KING

ETWORKING POST-MERGER

CAN YOU FACEBOOK YOUR WAY TO NEW JOB?

A TWITTER SUCCESS STORY

BE USEFUL, NOT PUSHY, PLEADING OR SHY

I recently heard the best suggestion for how to do great networking.

I was speaking to a group of about 100 professionals who are looking for work. In the past, I myself have recommended "qualified networking." If you were pursuing a specific job, I suggested your phone call go something like this:

"Say, Suzy, how's it going? Hey, did you hear that IBM is hiring somebody in your position over in the Davenport branch? Hey, I also noticed that your company is hiring somebody for my role. Yeah, it's true! Do you know who the real decision maker is on that one? I'd sure appreciate if you could give me a 'warm introduction' by e-mail … Thanks Suzy!"

But after my chat, a pretty sharp woman outlined for me her strategy for qualified networking. And I have to say, it is even better advice and takes my suggested phone call to Suzy one step further. She said, "When I find a job, and I have a contact or connection at that company, I'll send them an e-mail asking for help with that job. I include the name of the hiring manager, the job ID number, title, location, and specifically the fact that I've already sent in my information through TheLadders on such-and-such a date. I've discovered that the easiest way for them to brush you off is to tell you to go through the application process, so I make it abundantly clear that I've specifically complied with the system already."

I thought this was excellent. Why? Well, which e-mail comes across to you as a candidate who is taking the job search more seriously?

"I'm interested in this job and I think I'm a great fit. Here's my resume, and I'd really appreciate your help."

Or:

"I can contribute to your company immediately in the role of VP, Corporate. If you could help me get in contact with Sam Waller, who is the hiring manager for this position, I'd really appreciate it. The Job ID number is TLC-1234 and it's the VP, Corporate position in New York, N.Y. I applied for it on Sept. 9, but just in case, I am re-attaching my resume."

Being this specific is a big help to everybody who wants to help or hire you. Obviously, they know the job title and job ID number of their own job. That's not why you're mentioning it. Being specific and providing details shows the hiring manager that you are serious and committed. The more specific you are and the more details you provide, the better. You'll come across as a thorough person who has thoroughly thought through this particular job and thoroughly believes that you are qualified for it.

And that is a fantastic way to stand out.

Many senior job seekers employ networking tools that span at least three centuries. Laptops, iPads or Netbooks jostle with cell phones, spiral-bound notebooks and assorted pens.

You might be in a funk all day because your BlackBerry's on the fritz, but you know that the batteries will never run out on your leather-bound Franklin Covey organizer.

In short, today's job search requires all the resources possible to keep on track and in touch, whether the technology behind it was invented by Gutenberg or Gates. While you should never give up on a tool that still works for you just to prove you're trendy, now is the definitely the time to try new tricks that won't crimp your style.

Used correctly, social-networking tools can help extend your reach, but there's no substitute for traditional face-to-face events, either one on one or in groups. Whether you've never logged on to a social network or you're ready to hone your professional edge online, we'll set you straight on what you need to tend your professional network.

Crash! Pick Up Those Network Pieces

SERVICES LIKE THELADDERS are not only good to find job openings, they also provide tremendous insight into what potential employers are thinking and what kinds of skills they need, according to Esther G. She used the service in conjunction with her networking skills to find a new job as a lawyer in financial services.

"I tried to read between the lines and see what they're really looking for, beyond the bullet lists of requirements, and analyze what that implies for the firm," Esther says. "My approach was to create my own job by understanding what they really needed, then showing them that I could add value."

Create a group of peers—people you might even compete with for similar jobs—and make a pact to help each other out, advises Job Doctor International founder Jim Villwock. If you spot a job you like, tell the others, and get them to do the same. Who gets the job depends on chemistry and specific background, but pooling your information can expand your search capability 500 percent.

Generosity toward others in your network is the key to making the network work. "People are happy to help each other, but they don't like when you just call up looking for something, like it's a one-way street," Villwock says. "They don't like feeling taken advantage of."

Use the Soft Approach in Networking

HIRING MANAGERS already feel pressure from the financial situation of their companies, so don't add to the pressure. "I called them up and asked them how they're doing," Esther says. "I asked if there was anything I can do to help, and sometimes they mentioned something, but mostly I thought ahead of time what I could offer—services, references, whatever. If they were going on a trip to India, I gave them pages of tips on where to eat, what to do. It took a lot of research, but whatever I had, I gave. In the process I got three other people jobs. That extended my network even further, and those people will remember me."

Can You Facebook Your Way to a New Job?

IN THE OLD DAYS, "networking" meant hours calling every contact in your Rolodex; paging through the directories of every professional organization you could join; going to breakfast seminars, lunch-time speaking events, happy hours and board meetings to press the flesh—anything to make real-time, one-on-one contact with someone who might know someone who might be hiring.

The tools of the networking trade are changing and moving online, where e-mail, IM and social-networking Web sites such as LinkedIn, Facebook, and some specific to industry and career are the means to make new contacts and interact with current ones.

A social-networking Web site is essentially a fancy, online address book that allows you to see what your contacts are doing and connect to their contacts. The medium allows users to quickly expand their reach, putting them in touch with industry allies and hiring managers miles from home and in different companies and verticals. It's also an easy place to track relationships and promote yourself to a willing audience.

But how much use are online social networks to an executive seeking a job, and which ones are worth the effort?

"LinkedIn should be part of your strategy, but not in the way you might expect a good social-networking site to be," says Robert Neelbauer, owner of StaffMagnet.com, a Washington, D.C.-based recruitment consultancy. Rather then sitting at your PC clicking your way to a new job, use Web sites as the launch pad for traditional social networking. Pressing the flesh and phone calls remain the most intimate way to bond with the contacts in your network.

"If you're only looking at LinkedIn for lead generation or hunting down candidates for jobs, it's a valuable tool," he says. "But if you send a message to someone through LinkedIn, they may not respond to it for days or even weeks."

Neelbauer is particularly critical of LinkedIn. Although a frequent user almost from its launch in May 2003, he complains that the site has become watered down by millions of users and thousands of recruiters who have flooded the system with resumes and job posts and fill their networks with contacts they barely know. Neelbauer says he prefers other sites, especially Facebook, which gives users much greater control over who is in their network and sees their information. Facebook therefore tends to make in-network contacts more immediate for members, he says.

Don't Ignore the Web

WHILE ONLINE NETWORKING won't replace the handshake, you can't discount it entirely. Its role in job hunting specifically has become so central for recruiters and hiring managers that job seekers are severely handicapping themselves by not participating.

"If you're a recruiter and you're not using LinkedIn and Facebook or Twitter, I don't know what you're using," says Lindsay Olson, a partner at Paradigm Staffing.

Olson says social networking plays at least some role in the hiring process for more than 60 percent of the positions she fills. "LinkedIn, particularly, is the first place people go to look for candidates. When I get a name, that's where I look first to get a little more background on someone before I talk to them."

Online social networking is to networking what e-mail is to handwritten letters. It's just faster and a lot more convenient. Rather than meeting people one at a time at a conference to trade cards or calls once a year, social networks let you do something with those contacts. Put those people in a social-networking list, and you have the opportunity to learn more about them and let them get to know you in a low-key way.

"Social networking and marketing and job searching is all about getting yourself out there," says Paul Gillin of Paul Gillin Communications. Friends' networks can show you who's changing jobs, which means a job just opened up at their old company that you can go for that hasn't been posted yet. And [it] can help you get introduced to people closer to that job than you might have gotten otherwise."

Three Degrees of Separation

JOB SEEKER Jim Nash used LinkedIn not only to get a new job but also to do it in a foreign field where he had relatively few direct contacts. Nash has been a writer and editor at news, business and technology publications. He was the editorial director of NBC Universal's Sci-Fi Channel Web site and a former metro editor at the *Chicago Tribune*. But he wanted to follow his core interests into medical or science publishing, preferably with a nonprofit.

"I did know a few people at science publications, and that was helpful," Nash says. "The good thing about social networking was that if I knew nobody in an industry, I could still look at all the people who were related to me and the people they knew to find people in the area I wanted, so I could call them. I was casual about it but was clear that I was looking, and almost everybody I approached was happy either to talk to me or introduce me to someone else."

Nash landed his current job—Web managing editor at Mount Sinai Medical Center in New York—through three degrees of separation. One of his contacts had introduced him to another contact, who introduced him to his boss. The employer educated Nash on how and where medical organizations might be able to use Web-publishing savvy and eventually hired Nash himself. "Once we made that contact, it seemed like things moved really quickly," says Nash. "I contacted my current boss as the friend-of-a-friend-of-a-friend, and it just worked out."

But not everyone is comfortable introducing themselves to strangers, even when the strangers are online and the job seeker has a lot of experience at marketing and

Nash contacted a friend-of-a-friend-of-a-friend, who ultimately hired him. "Once we made that contact, things moved very quickly."

115

selling. Susan U. has a profile on LinkedIn but is reluctant to use it aggressively.

"The majority of people I know are not on it," she says. "So the people that would be contacting me on it are not likely to be close colleagues. None of my friends are really using LinkedIn to find jobs, and people who want me to use it seem to want to use my contacts. It seems more a way for business building than for networking."

Don't Ignore the Real World

DOING IT PROPERLY MEANS marrying your offline network to your online network, says Isabel Walcott Hilborn, owner of Strategic Internet Consulting and founder of SmartGirl.com, a 200,000-member social network for teenage girls.

Hilborn recommends a job seeker use the contacts he makes offline to build out his online social network, but then return to the offline sources when it comes time to make a job connection. For instance, when you find a job, online or off, don't just e-mail your resume or apply online, she says. "If you've taken the time to develop your network and keep those connections live, you can type in a keyword and find you have three friends who work there or know someone who does," she says. "Then you can write to your contact, ask if they'd forward this to their friend and ask her to submit your resume. It's almost impossible for HR to ignore a resume that's submitted from someone inside, and they usually get paid if they refer someone who gets hired, so it works out really well."

Even an interview that doesn't work out can extend your network and lead to opportunities you might not have had otherwise, Nash says.

"I'd always try to talk on the phone or meet people I made contact with," he says. "If they didn't have a job available, or it wasn't a match for some reason, I'd ask if I could link to them on LinkedIn and look through their contacts so I could write back in a week or two and say, 'Thanks for meeting with me; it was really great, and would you mind recommending me or introducing me to this other person?' And they were almost always fine with that."

It requires the same attention and interest in relationship building as traditional networking, Hilborn concludes.

"When someone changes their picture, you can comment on it, or when they put up a note about having had a hard day, you can commiserate or offer suggestions," Hilborn says. "And if in the past you've sent three e-mails to Maria, you are on her radar screen, so when you send an e-mail to all your contacts saying your company is doing a round of layoffs and you're on the list, she's going to respond, where if you just had her business card, she wouldn't even know you.

"Half an hour on Facebook once a week is all you'd need to keep that social network totally thriving," she says. "You have to pick and choose the things [to which] you respond to make them personal. But tiny little outreaches are quick; they take time over the long term, but one at a time, they're pretty quick. And it lets you stay in touch with a much larger community than you otherwise could."

Social-Networking Etiquette: Mind Your Manners

SOCIAL-NETWORKING WEB SITES have become an indispensable part of the job search. As your relationships move online, it's easy to track and manage your contacts and connections. Unfortunately, it's also easy to forget your social skills. Ignoring a contact's "hello" feels less harsh when it's done from 3,000 miles away. Sharing a racy joke with the group seems harmless when it's done on your mobile phone between interviews. But snubs still sting, and tawdry remains tactless.

According to social-networking experts, everything you need to succeed in the medium, you learned in kindergarten. "They're the same social rules as anywhere else," says Olson, who uses social networking to identify potential recruits and vet candidates once their names have come up. "There's a very thin line between keeping in touch and blatant self-promotion. Stepping over that line will really turn people off."

The key is to keep the other person in mind and go out of your way to be both polite and helpful before you need help yourself, says Gillin. "The etiquette is that you help people out and then when you need it, they help you out in return."

LinkedIn provides built-in ways for people to contribute. Members can submit questions to the group, plead for jobs, post openings at their company and recommend a friend or colleague. Providing answers, resources or tips; passing along a resume; or making an introduction can build social equity.

Be Useful, Not Pushy, Pleading or Shy

TWITTER. THE MICROBLOGGING SITE that allows users to post 140-character messages that can be read by members in their network, has been growing in popularity among everyone—including job hunters. Some use Twitter messages (often called "tweets") to broadcast their location or status on a project, or just to say "hello" to a friend. Resourceful job seekers have made Twitter part of their self-promotion engine. But be sure not to inundate followers with a constant stream of boasts, Olson says. Blatant self-promotion or begging for work will turn off your audience.

If you're using a site like Twitter or Facebook to promote yourself, make sure you slip in your sales pitch between useful information like articles from trade publications, white papers on your industry and helpful advice.

Don't hesitate to ask for introductions and expect to do the same for others. It feels like trading, but it's really just part of networking. Asking someone to write you a recommendation, for example, is fair game. "It's a give-to-get situation," says Gillin. "Often when you write a recommendation, even unsolicited, you'll get one in return." But don't shake down your contacts. Most people feel good if they can help you out, especially if your request isn't blatant self-promotion.

Don't Be a Creep

Recruiters routinely search social-networking sites and many will hold photos of youthful hijinks against you. Eliminate anything questionable from public sites during the job search.

CONSIDER THE "CREEP FACTOR" when calling someone you've researched online or through social networks, Gillin says. "If someone contacted you out of thin air and had all this information about you that you didn't know was out there, that might creep you out," Gillin says. "The way around that is to be open with who you are and where you got the information. Say, 'ZoomInfo says you used to work at this company while I was there too, and I was hoping to make a connection.'

"Adopt a professional manner; it's a business contact, and you're reaching out in a business sense," he says. "Don't make it overly personal."

A public profile can put you on someone's radar or keep you there. Whether you submitted your resume cold or you were in for an interview, a connection on a social network and frequent activity can keep your name in a recruiter or contact's ear. "People aren't going to remember me because I made one recruiting call to them five years ago," Olson says, "but if they see me posting things all the time, they're going to know who I am when I call."

Above all, behave. As any number of college students and Miss America contestants can tell you, it's bad form to record your indiscretions and post the evidence. Embarrassing photos or remarks can surface during your job search. Recruiters and hiring managers routinely search social-networking sites for background information, and many will hold photos of youthful hijinks against candidates.

Get Googled, Get Found

WEB DEVELOPERS DON'T RELY ON LUCK to drive readers to their Web site. They use search engine optimization (SEO) to increase the likelihood search engines will showcase their Web pages. Your profiles on LinkedIn and other social networks should be no different. Make sure recruiters can find you.

SEO relies on the concept that the more prominently a Web page appears in search results, the more searchers will visit the page. Optimizing your profile pushes it toward the top. SEO marketers—a budding job classification—add keywords, which are the terms that are most likely to be queried by a Web searcher interested in the topic you are trying to promote—in this case, your career. If you want to be noticed by anyone who needs a database administrator with MySQL experience, your profile should include those specific terms, instead of more generic or less descriptive terms like "DBA" or "database admin" and any specific languages or skills the recruiter might search for.

Choosing the right network for your profile can also help. While Facebook might be a larger, more useful network for your profession, LinkedIn is particularly well-positioned for Google searches.

Promote Your Ambitions, Expand Your Network

NOW THAT YOU'RE FINISHED optimizing your profile for search, make sure it matches what you want to do, not just what you've done. Choose words that match your aspirations, not just your history. "If I were a digital-marketing person and I wanted to move into an SEO job, I'd put it in as an area of interest or whatever," Olson says. "As long as I got those keywords into the text so I could be found on those searches."

LinkedIn may be the most widely known and used social network purely for business contacts. However, it isn't right for everyone or every situation. You may run into situations where you identify a company or individual you need to contact and use other searches to find e-mail addresses, phone numbers or other information to get you closer to that contact. ZoomInfo, Spock and other business-information aggregation sites are great places to gather information about your target companies or hiring managers.

The biggest mistake most people make using LinkedIn, Facebook and social networks is that they don't complete their profiles with all the information about their experience, skills and miscellaneous information that could be relevant; what's more, they don't pursue contacts. Omitting information makes it difficult for recruiters to find your profile and hard for you to connect to new opportunities through your contacts.

Remember, your network doesn't build itself. You have to take advantage of the opportunities to expand your reach. When you meet someone at an event or on the phone, ask if they mind if you link to them, then do it. "It's exactly like real life, like a virtual water cooler where you talk to your friends or co-workers," Hilborn says. "If you're the kind of person who never needs anything—a job or a plumber or advice on how to raise your baby—go ahead and skip the whole social-networking thing. But if you ever need anything from anyone else, social networks can help you."

Job-Hunting Tools

IF THE WEB HAS TRANSFORMED the way you do your job, you can bet your bottom dollar it has changed the way you find a job. At its most basic, the Web is an encyclopedia of reference material to help you educate yourself about your intended market, region or company. If you're ready to take a more active role online, you can employ some of the social-networking tools to manage your contacts and relationships as you hunt for work. And for the creative and brave, the Web offers a route to promote yourself in a way a paper resume can't.

Here are a few of the resources you should know about:

SlideShare

It's like YouTube for PowerPoint presentations. Users make slideshows and upload them to SlideShare for all to see. Some uninventive job seekers have posted simple one- and two-page slides of their actual paper resume. But a few slick and creative examples back up bullet points on the resume with figures and graphs.

YouTube

A few adventurous souls are already posting video resumes that are essentially a sales pitch. Most job seekers simply read their resume aloud into the camera, but the format might be the right fit for the right candidate or the right industry.

Google

Never walk into an interview cold. Do your homework. There's no better place to start than Google. Is the company performing well? What's the CFO's name? Check a publicly traded company's financials and basic information on Google Finance. Is the board of directors under indictment? Did the new drug win FDA approval? Follow articles and blogs that mention the company on Google News.

GlassDoor

This is a free site for deep research on many companies. It will generally give you more detail than what you'll find on Google.

Harris InfoSource

Detailed company profiles are available for a fee.

Twitter

See what people are saying about you or a potential employer.

Old Media

To research a company's less-tangible qualities, like, "Is it a nice place to work?" rely on the good old news media. *Fortune's* "100 Best Companies to Work For" survey is exhaustive. Your company may not be on here, but the survey explores such topics as best cafeteria and most unusual perks. Sources like *Working Mother* magazine's "Best Companies" survey profiles companies from the perspective of its specific audience.

Networking Post-Merger

A LAYOFF IS NEVER EASY. Nevertheless, if your previous job was focused on studying the maze of social-networking sites and figuring out how to use them best, you'd be way ahead of the game.

At least, Randy G. hoped he would. In 2009 he was the vice president and research director at a market-research firm, in charge of a group of 40 analysts. They brought in more than $15 million per year by creating reports that measured, and often changed the direction of, huge markets in consumer and digital media.

The shock of his layoff left Randy without an immediate plan. "Most jobs are gotten through networking—knowing people, talking to people, and a big percentage of that today is done through social networking as well as in person." Like millions of other out-of-work executives, Randy found it's hard to separate online and offline networking.

After all, we now rely on online job boards, social-networking sites and mobile devices to make connections. Knowing people, talking to people, and finding and capitalizing on job leads, now takes place largely online.

A Twitter Success Story

RANDY STARTED CLOSE TO HOME. He signed up for groups on LinkedIn that focused on market research, consumer electronics, mobile and other technology areas in which he had some experience, and for groups formed by recruiters he'd worked with in the past. Members of the groups alerted him to a series of job openings that had either been posted only in inaccessible places or not at all—opportunities in the "background job market" that he would never have seen without a connection to specific parts of the industry in which he'd worked for years.

"Vertical-market groups and networks really have become one of the most effective, most reliable sources for that kind of job information," according to social networking expert Gillin. "A lot of people think they don't have the time or expertise to use industry-specific or at-large social-networking sites," Gillin explains. "But if you make yourself savvy—and it's not hard—in how to use Plaxo and LinkedIn and Twitter and vertical networks, you can do a lot."

Randy focused his job search on one: Twitter. In his former job, he maintained a Twitter feed where customers could follow his analysis of industry issues in the news. He realized he could leverage this and show his value to potential employers by compiling and analyzing information for his followers.

"That kept me in contact with a lot of people who [had] sought me out. People [were] saying they didn't have any openings right now, but offering or raising the possibility of some consulting work that might last through the summer, and [saying] we could talk more in the fall," Randy remembers. "Especially in July and August, when the number of job postings went way down, I built a network of people with different specialties I could turn to on a freelance basis to fulfill some of the more complicated engagements."

This "push" strategy on Twitter resulted in most of his job contacts coming to him, rather than vice versa. "Mostly they came through Twitter or they searched on Linked In for people with certain skills and found me that way," he says.

Start With a Strategy, Not a Tool

TOO MANY JOB SEEKERS approach their social networks the wrong way when they're looking for a job. Some just march right out and broadcast, "I need a job. Can anyone help?"

"Desperation creates paralysis," says Ellen Gordon Reeves, author of *"Can I Wear My Nose Ring to the Interview?"* "People get a whiff of desperation, and it turns them off, for one thing. When people feel out of control, they'll say they're happy to do anything. When you say that, there's nothing in my brain [such as a contact] that I can use to help you. I have all these networks and contacts and resources, but if I don't have a clue what you're looking for, I don't know how to help you. When you approach people like that you're asking the helper or potential employer to do the digging to figure out how to help you."

The best approach is the same direct contact, web-of-trust method used in more traditional, in-person networking. "The most important thing is to have a strategy," Gillin says. "I'll go to events that people go to with the express purpose of networking for jobs and they haven't even thought about how I can help them. You can't put the tool first; you have to know what you're looking for and then use the tool—whether it's Twitter or LinkedIn or Plaxo or another service—to help you get there."

Reeves agrees. "You have to stop looking for a job and start looking for a person. If you ask a roomful of people how they got their jobs, 80 percent will say it was through some kind of referral. So you have to stop sending your resume into the black hole of cyberspace, and use the tools to research and find the companies and the job you're interested in and the person you should talk to about that job. Then you use social-networking tools to make that contact happen."

Good Strategies in Action

THAT BACKDOOR APPROACH works remarkably well, according to Aliza Freud, CEO of SheSpeaks.com, a word-of-mouth marketing start-up that enrolls women in a cooperative effort to make their voices heard to developers of the products they use.

Example 1: One candidate Freud recently hired got noticed by searching She-Speaks.com to get familiar with the company's approach, and also following Freud's own Twitter feed "to gain a better perspective on my thinking and hot buttons [as a potential employer]," Freud explains.

Example 2: Another researched the company and then used LinkedIn to find connections who could make the recommendations that helped make the candidate "stand out among hundreds of candidates" and eventually land the job.

Narrow Your Focus and Your Sources

"THE GENERAL JOB BOARDS are full of junk, so you have to find the ones that filter some of that out," advises David Schmidt, a Michigan-based 20-year PR and marketing veteran, who used TheLadders and followed several Twitter feeds to find job leads.

One problem is that Twitter—with its tweets and retweets and tweetups—is alien-sounding and overwhelming to the uninitiated, according to Rick Stom-

> "You have to stop looking for a job and start looking for a person."

phorst, a director of operations and development at Econstruction.com who is highly rated by the LinkedIn community as an expert on the use of social networks. A huge number of new jobs are posted through Twitter, but the number of feeds is so enormous that it's hard to find them, he explains.

One option is to identify a small number of companies you want to work with or recruiters who work in your industry, search for the Twitter feeds of executives from those companies, and follow them. You learn a lot about their priorities and methods, often hear about their job postings first, and get yourself instant credibility as a longtime follower of their tweets.

Corporate Social Networks

FINDING JOB LISTINGS is one thing, finding them credible is another. Select-Minds has become one of the leading software providers for social networks owned and controlled by specific companies and organizations, like alumni associations and industry groups. According to Kate Lukach, director of marketing for Select-Minds, when a company implements this "closed network" software, job seekers get a good source of leads at a company where they're already a known commodity, so it improves their chances of landing a job. And it drastically cuts the cost of recruiting, vetting and training new employees.

> **Social-networking tools can make offline contacts happen.**

Internal, corporate social networks compete with less controlled, sometimes less focused alumni networks or social networks such as LinkedIn, Ning.com and others. But they're qualitatively different. Lukach explains that each user's real name and work history is accessible via hyperlink when they comment within the closed network. This all but guarantees members behave as if they're in a company conference room, not on the wild Web.

Job seeker Schmidt can relate. "It's still the Wild West out there, but the resources you can find are getting so deep and rich you can do amazing things," Schmidt says. "The challenge becomes which ones are worth the time, because you can't ignore personal contacts and phone calls and just sit in front of the computer all day."

New Opportunities for Older Execs

AS OLDER WORKERS stave off retirement or re-enter the job search, many are turning their age to their advantage and overcoming age discrimination. Pete K. exemplifies this new breed of job seeker. He is 70 years old. He's had three distinct careers and retired once already. But right now he's looking for work.

The percentage of workers age 50 and older has risen dramatically as more Americans remain longer in the work force and the job search. Like Pete, many are re-entering the job search after resigning from it once already. He retired six years ago, but felt unproductive without a job. "I'm a business guy; I need to be in business."

For others, the decision to postpone or cancel retirement after it has begun is financial. There are many factors that prompt this move: Your mortgage has become more costly, your retirement savings were depleted by the decline in the stock market, your adult children now need support or your aging parents have their own trouble making ends meet.

The result is a work force and pool of job seekers older than ever and desperate to overcome age discrimination in the hunt for work.

Dan Kohrman, a senior attorney at AARP who oversees age-discrimination cases says, "Whenever there's a downturn even much milder than the recent one, the proportion of workers who lose their jobs who are older workers is greater, is disproportionate. And although older workers [may sometimes be costlier than other candidates], that's almost never the explanation."

Proving Age Discrimination

THE EQUAL EMPLOYMENT OPPORTUNITY COMMISSION has reported a significant recent increase in age-discrimination complaints. And those complaints are just for those who already have a job. Age discrimination on the job search is less visible and rarely reported, Kohrman says. "When you're applying for jobs, it's frequently hard to tell if you've been discriminated against," he explains. "You can get an interview; you can get a friendly interview, but you can also get an interviewer who takes one look at your resume and your appearance and says to themselves, 'Too old,' and you'll never know."

AARP conducts sting operations to test hiring organizations for age discrimination. "The evidence seems pretty clear and dramatic that the treatment of job applicants is different for older workers, given all other circumstances being equal," Kohrman says. "But it's hard to detect."

Age vs. Experience

MANY OLDER JOB SEEKERS think of their experience, age and maturity as an advantage in the marketplace when competing for jobs against younger candidates,

HIRED! POST-MERGER, HR VP'S NETWORK PAYS OFF

From the time Rick Joers got the news that his employer, JP Morgan, would be acquiring Bear Stearns, he sensed that he might be working toward eliminating his own job. At the same time, he was too busy helping to merge the two companies to do any serious work on his resume or start a job search.

Joers, a vice president of human resources at JP Morgan for eight years, started working toward a layoff on a Sunday afternoon. "My boss called me in on Sunday, March 16. I worked until 1 a.m. that day on the acquisition. It was the start of a six-month project. I knew even then that there was a chance I might not have a job when the merger was complete. But we were working long hours; there was a lot to do. I didn't have time to do my work and search for another job."

Indeed, he got word by June that he would be losing his job, and in September he left JP Morgan. Compounding his concern was the fact that, at the age of 58, he had not done a job search in a very long time.

He thought about ways to attack the market and determine what he could offer employers. At the same time, he decided to open up his search to Northern California as well as New York.

"I did a lot of work in mergers and acquisitions and global organizations. I had some expertise in employee relations," he says.

"So I started looking at companies other than financial services that could use those strengths. And my partner was working for a company based out of Sonoma. So my strategy was to target my search in Silicon Valley because one of my major projects had been supporting global technology."

NEW NETWORKING CHANNELS

He didn't have any professional contacts in the San Francisco Bay area, but he did have a network on LinkedIn that he tapped: The Gay, Lesbian, Bisexual, Transgender group had many members who were professionals in the technology field. He was surprised at how many people were willing to talk to him. At the same time, Joers joined TheLadders, hoping to find job listings in the Bay area. "I set alerts for Northern California and New York City, and targeted my search in those two locations," he says. "You've got to have a lot of quivers and a lot of arrows to hand."

In the end, his network came through for him. A recruiter placed an ad on TheLadders for a position at the Royal Bank of Scotland. "I contacted the recruiter, and they called me the next day," he says. "I went on LinkedIn, and a woman who had done consulting for JP Morgan when I was there was now working at RBS. I e-mailed her that

I was applying for the position; she wrote to tell me that the position reports to her! Since she was the most influential decision maker, it was helpful to have someone who knew me."

Several rounds of interviews beginning in November ended with a job offer in January. Joers is now technical partner at Royal Bank of Scotland, with oversight of employee relations. His new job, based in Stamford, Conn., requires him to commute over an hour each way, but he's happy to be working and to have found a job as quickly as he did.

Looking back, he's glad he gave some other options a try. "It would have been fun to take the plunge and go to San Francisco," Joers says. "I had a six-month severance, but it was going to take time for me to find something there. And I didn't want to tap into savings."

And while his two-pronged strategy made sense, he says he learned to not underestimate himself or his skills, even in a tough economic market. "I had the mistaken belief that there was no way to go back to a bank or financial-services firm because of what was happening in the market," Joers says. "The power of your resume, especially if you have built a career in the market, should not be overlooked. My global experience was very helpful, [as was] my employee-relations experience and M&A experience. In the end, it worked for me."

and sometimes it is. But as one veteran with 30 years of work behind him says of his recent job search, "For the vast majority of my conversations and interviews, I think I was fighting an uphill battle."

Pete also thought his age was a handicap, despite his energy. "The young are ruling the world, and they really think they know it all so they don't need us. I've never personally been confronted with my age, but I know they figure it out, and they just don't call," he says. "It's a shame because I'm on top of my game, and I'm pretty bright, and I know there are a lot of guys and gals who can offer an awful lot to some of these young people who really ... have no idea and think they know everything themselves."

Part of the reason older workers face trouble, Kohrman says, is the stereotypes employers have. "[Some employers think] if you have a long career and a lot of experience, you have to get a salary equal to the highest salary you've ever had, which is not true." The perception, he says, "is that if you can't equal the best job you've ever had, you'll never be happy."

Tips for Beating the "Age Filter"

SO HOW DO YOU GET THROUGH THE FILTER that seems to screen out older job candidates? The best way is not to make it an issue early, says AARP's Kohrman. "What we say is, 'Don't invite consideration of your age' because it's going to happen in the ordinary course in many instances anyway."

One way to keep from getting screened out early is by tuning your resume. Eliminate the year from any degrees and early jobs and focus on more recent experience. Don't be deceptive or dishonest, but "don't offer very old experience on your resume, even if it's impressive," Kohrman says. "At some point, the very length of your resume may count against you."

You may want to narrow the scope of your resume to show specific expertise and focus on jobs that match what makes you unique. "It wasn't until toward the end of the process that I started to recognize the value of my uniqueness and started ignoring the other things that were out there," says Chuck Jordan, a job seeker who had retired from his job as a technology salesman but decided to re-enter the work force just six months later. He started focusing on jobs that played to his strengths as an expert in selling to the federal government and landed a position soon after.

But of course, you can't hide your age at the interview, and there's nothing that precludes a potential employer from asking your age. "If an employer is really digging into those age issues," Kohrman says, "try some gentle way of fending off that line of questioning.

"Give something from your background that demonstrates that [you] have attri-

butes consistent with vigor and energy and creativity and initiative and insight—
all those things that some employers think only younger workers have—that counters the stereotypes," Kohrman advises.

Getting the Job When You're Overqualified

IN THE PAST TEN YEARS, a movement called "downshifting" sprung up among
older professionals who sought to simplify their lives and have more time for family, pet projects and personal fulfillment off the clock. Then a tanking economy
brought a whole new spin to downshifting. Senior-level professionals accustomed
to high salaries lowered their expectations for their next positions in hopes of just
making ends meet.

Call it downshifting. Call it "re-careering." It's a genuine phenomenon, regardless of whether it's voluntary or the child of necessity. More and more people over
50 are making career changes to new jobs in new industries, in full-time, part-
time, and contract or self-employed positions.

In a buyer's market, however, employers are much more exacting about finding
the precise fit for their requirements. Getting in front of a hiring manager when
you're clearly overqualified for the position requires some feats of repackaging.
"Many older workers are ready to give up the long-time grind and look for stimulat-
ing jobs with flexible schedules as they begin the process toward retirement," says
Susan Reinhard, senior vice president of the AARP Public Policy Institute.

A report from the University of Michigan for the National Institute on Aging,
Health and Retirement Study confirms this tendency. From 1992 to 2006, the
analysis tracked a sample of workers who were ages 51 to 55 during that timeframe.
Among those studied, 28.8 percent of men and 24.3 percent of women changed
careers after age 50. Most made the move for less money—$6 an hour less, on aver-
age—and were less likely to have retirement benefits or health insurance in their
new jobs. Among those who changed jobs after age 50 and were managers, 35 percent went from management to non-management positions.

The benefit of a job with less responsibility? Most respondents reported that their
new positions were less stressful and offered more flexible hours, and 91.3 percent
said they enjoyed their work, up from 79 percent in the old job.

"The current downturn presents a real bump in the road," Reinhard adds, "but,
for the future, the findings are a welcome signal that workers 50 and over can really
enjoy themselves while remaining productive in a vibrant economy."

That bump in the road has created a strong incentive to go back to work, says
Bruce Lee, a spokesman for Mercer, a global HR and financial-consulting company. "If you're 25, even if you had a big loss in your 401(k) balance you could still

be in good shape if you're a disciplined saver. Some of the folks who might be 55, 60—they just don't have time on their side."

Whatever your motive for scaling back your salary requirements, the challenge remains the same: compelling employers to believe you're ready to commit to a job that's considerably lower paid and less senior than your last one.

"There is an automatic assumption time and time again, where someone who was making $300,000 a few years ago is interested in a $150,000 job," says Randy Hain, managing partner at Bell Oaks Executive Search in Atlanta. "Clients automatically think, 'There's no way that'd work.' And yet you and I know, in this economy, that'd work—they'd take [even] $100,000."

That reaction isn't universal, however, according to Colleen O'Neill, a principal at Mercer. "Smart companies are not wasting a good recession. They're saying, 'OK, there's this glut of really top talent out there looking for jobs.' And what we've heard just in some recent roundtables with companies across different industries, particularly industries that are still in better shape during a recessionary time—like in health care or certain kinds of consumer products that haven't been hurt as badly—a lot of them have said, 'Wow, there are about 40,000 people from financial services out there looking for jobs. ... I've picked some of those people up knowing that I never would have been able to recruit them to my industry three years ago.' "

Sell Yourself Short

IF YOUR EXPERIENCE is in a troubled industry, you may have to find a whole new way to package it, Hain says. "I know a guy who was senior in the insurance industry," he says. "He ended up taking a project-manager job with a small company that saw some value in his leadership skills. But he couldn't find anything related to his experience. I see that a lot with anyone related to real estate right now, or home lending, mortgages. ... There's just nothing to be found. Either they take a job in a new industry, or they take anything they can in their industry to survive."

O'Neill says she believes hiring managers tend to be much more flexible about cross-industry moves today. "When we're talking to recruiting managers, they're very open, and they know that even that highly qualified candidate might have been making much more than they're offering today.

"And then certainly, I think people have a different mindset: It's not necessarily going to hurt their long-term prospects that they have something else to add in their portfolio, that there was some period of time that they worked in a different industry, had a different job—we're kind of in a different place than we were the last recession," she says. "People know they're going to have many jobs over the course of their working life. From an employers' standpoint, I think people are very open to it."

Where to Find Smaller Opportunities

EVEN SO, FINDING A JOB—even one that pays significantly less, with less responsibility—is still a challenge. Knowing where to look and who to approach can significantly reduce the length of a search. Look for companies that are hungry for talent. The best opportunities for anyone looking to downshift are often small companies

HIRED!
RETIRED SALESMAN RETURNS TO THE JOB-SEARCH FRAY

Chuck Jordan, 56, was retired and looked forward to living the good life after 28 years as a federal sales rep for a communications company based in California. But as the economy slowed and his 401(k) shrank, Jordan, who lives near Sacramento, began to get nervous. After a five-month sabbatical, an opportunity for a high-level sales position at Northrop-Grumman opened up and Jordan went back to the work force.

After only a year, however, he says he was back to square one, as the entire division for which he worked closed. More than 700 people lost their jobs that day. Here's how he rebounded—again.

MAKING THE PITCH

Jordan's first instinct, as with many job seekers, was to blanket the known universe with resumes and cover letters and hope that sheer quantity would sway the odds in his favor. "If you looked through my e-mail, there are probably over a hundred different versions of my resume and cover letter," he says.

He signed up for "all the different job-search sites," scanned local newspapers and magazines, and networked furiously in attempts to land a position. One incident, however, offered him an astounding perspective and permanently changed the way he went about his job search.

"I'd applied for a job I found in the paper with a solar-energy products manufacturing company, and I realized one day when I was out that I was right around the corner from the address. I decided to stop by," he says. What he found was a nearly empty office space and a lone receptionist.

He explained his situation and asked if he could get some additional information about the job, the benefits and salary. The receptionist informed him that the company had received more than 300 applications for the position, and that only $35,000 had been budgeted for the position. "That was really sobering," Jordan says. "A job that wasn't that great, with lousy pay, and they had over 300 applications."

But that experience turned out to be a blessing in disguise. He realized that it made more sense to rein in his search and home in on specific markets and companies with which he knew his skills and experience aligned. "You'd think that it would make more sense to apply for anything at all you could possibly do, but in reality, if you don't differentiate yourself in some way, one of

that are still growing and have a need for leaders, but don't have the ability to promote leaders from within. Companies to avoid include those large enough to promote from within and find what they're looking for in their own staff.

"I would stay away from the Fortune 1000 companies—the small to midsize companies are your best bet," Hain says. "Because the bigger companies—the Cokes, Home Depots, GEs—they've got enormous workforces with a need to promote from within. But the small and midsize companies are always looking to buy talent."

To illustrate his point, Hain cites a recent candidate with whom he worked. "There was a gentleman who was a VP of sales for a division of GE Healthcare, and he got downsized along with the rest of his unit. He wound up taking a job as a director of business development for a new division of a company in Atlanta that

those other people will get a job and you won't," Jordan says.

DEAL OR NO DEAL?

As a sales representative with a career focused on the government market, Jordan says he'd been under pressure most of his working life to move to the East Coast. But he was adamant that he could do what he loved and stay where he was. For more than a year, Jordan was employed at a number of companies in California. His first position was with a company that did work for the State of California itself, where he was assured he'd be the only salesperson working with the state. When he started the job, he realized they'd left out some crucial information.

"It was a big culture shock," says Jordan, who'd worked much of his career in business-casual environments or from a virtual home office. And, he says, he discovered that far from being the head salesperson at the firm, he'd been hired to handle

overflow work from an existing employee. Needless to say, it wasn't a fit.

"I thought, 'OK, I work in a cube, I have to wear a tie, and I'm a second-hand salesperson!' I realized shortly that it just wasn't gratifying," he says. After moving to another position, he encountered similar issues. "My next company hired me and rehired an employee who'd left the company some time earlier. He took over existing accounts in preferable sales territories, and I was given new accounts who'd never worked with the company before," Jordan says.

CLOSING THE SALE

After 13 months, Jordan signed up with TheLadders, which allowed him to fine-tune his search and weeded out positions and companies that didn't fit his criteria. "It did a lot of the qualifying and handled the elimination process for me," he says. "What was taking me ten hours a day was made so much simpler."

His refusal to give up or to give in paid off, when Jordan landed a position as senior account manager/consultant with Valencia, Calif.-based Nexus IS, which works on many federal government contracts.

Jordan says he's happy about the choices he made. While his base salary isn't as high as it was in previous jobs, Jordan's not complaining. He understands that base pay rates have declined because of the economy, and adds that he has no salary cap in his new position, so his total earnings are up to him,

Jordan says the key to surviving and thriving was tenacity and a positive attitude. "Once you realize that complaining and moaning aren't going to help, you just have to stick with it and never give up," Jordan says. "Once you get past that, fighting depression and suppressing the urge to just give up is the hardest part."

wanted to sell their services to hospitals.

"He was managing a team of 50, and now he's an individual contributor. But it's kind of exciting for him because he's starting a new business unit. He's the only guy doing the business development, and they hired him because of his relationships."

Volunteer Opportunities Pay Off

MANY IN THE RANKS of the unemployed have sought out volunteer work to pass the time and remain active in the absence of a 9-to-5 daily assignment. And some of those volunteers have found, by design or serendipity, that donating time and skills to a charity can be a ticket to employment.

Making such a transition takes planning. Job seekers who have leveraged charity work into full-time employment, executives who run nonprofit organizations and job-search experts all say that making the connection is not as simple as signing up to serve meals at the senior center. To turn volunteer work into employment requires a strategic decision about what organizations are most likely to help your career and what roles you can serve that will put you in a position to connect your volunteer service to full-time work. But don't discount your passion for a particular cause or group, they caution. Combining a strategic appraisal of your options and your heart's desire can lead to a job that nourishes your income and your soul.

Do What You Know

HERE'S JUST ONE EXAMPLE: After she was laid off, Jane B., a marketing professional in Massachusetts, thought long and hard about what she really wanted to do next. During college, she had done a work/study assignment and volunteered for the Massachusetts Society for the Prevention of Cruelty to Animals. When Jane lost her marketing job, she decided that animal welfare was her calling and went back to her MSPCA roots.

The difference this time: Jane saw volunteering at the agency as an opportunity to gain the experience and contacts she would need to secure a paying job. She approached the MSPCA about doing some pro bono marketing work. This move put her directly in front of the directors of marketing at the MSPCA agency she hoped might connect her to full-time work there or help her network to find another job. She never had the chance to test that tactic. She found her next job at a Web site focused on animal welfare through an online posting.

"While I was volunteering, I actually found the job ... online," says Jane. "One of the people who I was volunteering with had worked at the company previously. I said, 'Hey, do you know anyone whom I can show my resume to?' 'I'll send it,' she said, and the rest is history."

Jane volunteered at the MSPCA because she believed in the work it does, but she

5 WAYS TO PACKAGE YOURSELF FOR A SMALLER ROLE

Convincing an employer you'll savor a new role with a lower profile requires some serious self-branding. Randy Hain, managing partner at Bell Oaks Executive Search in Atlanta, suggests how.

1. Be a mentor. Market yourself as someone who can help mentor the next generation from inside the company. A lot of companies worry they don't have any mentors left. This kind of "come in, develop the next leaders and then bow out" approach can actually work.

2. Be a maven. Package yourself as a thought leader in a particular area of expertise. Use social-networking sites to demonstrate your knowledge.

Start to talk about your background. Project enthusiasm—and not your age!

3. Be a contractor. Approach companies as a consultant. Try a strategy like, "Hey look, I'm going to come in and take care of this project for you for six months, nine months, a year, then let's evaluate how I've done." This could be very attractive mid-career, as you get to avoid the grind of being part of the team.

4. Be honest with yourself. Evaluate what you really want out of the next five to 10 years of your career. Is it ego gratification, or do you want to make enough money to get to retirement? That's a tough evaluation for people

who've been flying high. Then evaluate what you have to offer. Ask yourself, "Do I have a Rolodex? Do I have a good reputation? Do I have a strong track record? Who's going to take my call, make introductions for me, or hire me?" Once you know all of that, gravitate toward identifying specific companies to approach.

5. Be flexible. It's key, especially early on in the job search, to project flexibility and get into a proper mindset. If you open yourself up to contributing, getting a fair income and really being convincing to a prospective employer, it goes a long way toward success.

volunteered in a role that she could leverage in her job search. It's why she volunteered to work in the marketing department and not as, say, a dog walker.

Choosing the right role for your charity work is key to connecting volunteer experience to full-time employment, says Rahul D. Yodh, an executive recruiter with Link Legal Search Group in Dallas. "If you volunteer in a situation where you can utilize your day-to-day business skills, then I think it's a great idea and a great way to further your career because you're essentially doing a job, not just sitting around. At the same time, you're building some contacts, and you never know where that will lead," Yodh says. "If you can get a high-enough level volunteering position, then that's probably the best route to take."

Leverage Your Pro Bono Network

VOLUNTEERING IS THE ROUTE Nate Towne traveled to a public-relations job in Madison, Wis., after relocating from Portland, Maine. When he found himself without a job or any business contacts in that part of the country, he decided to build his network by joining a local chapter of the Public Relations Society of America.

Not long afterward, Towne realized that the organization could greatly benefit from volunteers to help judge entries for a regional public relations awards program. The chairperson of the judging committee also happened to be the PR director of Madison's largest advertising firm, Hiebing, and Towne figured that volunteering couldn't hurt as a way to demonstrate his skills to a prominent figure in his profession.

"I realized what better chance will I have to demonstrate my skills in a PR setting than to actually work with people who are already employed at some big agencies and at big hiring companies here in Madison and around Madison?" Towne says. "I can show them that a) I'm willing to roll up my sleeves and work for no pay, and b) I'm a smart person who gets things done and has some opinions about how things should be done."

As luck would have it, Hiebing was hiring. "I was the first one called because they had already worked with me," Towne says. He was hired as public-relations counselor at Hiebing.

When Volunteering, Choose Your Charity Carefully

BOTH JANE AND NATE were strategic about choosing the organizations they volunteered for and the services they provided to those organizations. But that's not to say that you will easily have your pick of nonprofits, especially when you are offering up a specific set of business skills. Jane researched many nonprofit organizations, within and outside the animal-welfare area, and found that about half were interested in her marketing skills while half didn't really know what they could do with them.

Organizations such as VolunteerMatch.org and Idealist.org can help you find a good fit. The goal of VolunteerMatch, based in San Francisco, is "to help nonprofits reach their mission through effective volunteering," says Robert J. Rosenthal, VolunteerMatch's director of communications.

"The range of volunteer activities that are posted at VolunteerMatch really represents the spectrum of national and community service activities in this country, and that includes unskilled and skilled labor," he says. "As a result, a huge

percentage of people who do volunteer work as a strategy for career development and promotion are finding their opportunities in places like VolunteerMatch."

Towne wanted to help even after he had found a paying job in Madison. He is currently volunteering for HospiceCare, both because he believes strongly in the work the organization does and because it gives him a chance to network and gain experience. "I think volunteering is something important to do, and it helps round out my resume in the nonprofit sector," he says. "I volunteer time in the gardens. I'm doing non-business things, but I'm doing it with a lot of business leaders here in Madison."

In the end, any volunteer experience—no matter what your motivation going in—can be a valuable boost to your resume and can help you stand out from a growing crowd. The experience will likely be personally rewarding as well as professionally savvy.

"Get as much as you can out of the volunteering experience," says Theo Stripling, program associate with Literacy Volunteers of Illinois. "You never know when you're going to be presented with an opportunity. You may pick up another skill set along the way that makes you more marketable, and that's something that's very hard to do these days."

Volunteering Expands Network, Reveals Jobs

WHEN THE START-UP Brian Clark was working for—a mobile e-mail platform company—ran out of financing, Clark saw it as a chance to take some time off, relax and recharge. It was 2008, the economy was in relatively good shape, and he felt he could afford to spend time with his family. "I was relaxed about the job hunt," he says. "I thought I should enjoy some time off, because I didn't know when I'd get the chance again."

He ended up with a longer hiatus than he expected. A year longer.

His first instinct: Go to his network.

His second: Expand that network.

"I was working on the assumption that your network lasts about four months," he says. "After that, you've tapped that contact out. So you need to keep refreshing it." Clark's strategy: volunteer on local government committees in Thousand Oaks, Calif., the suburb of Los Angeles where he lives. He used his business-development expertise to assist the investment committee as well as a few nonprofits in the area. This helped the city government make decisions about which events and groups the city should provide with funds. "We'd go over applications, make sure applications were complete, and discuss the various options," Clark says.

In doing so he was able to expand his professional network. "I made a lot of business contacts; people who own or work at local companies or in Los Angeles," Clark says. "My goal was to stay in the L.A. area, so it was important to make contact with people in the community."

Clark found that working on community committees also helped him avoid isolation. "Expanding my network was not only healthy from a business standpoint but from an emotional standpoint as well," he says. "Being unemployed can be isolating. But volunteering, having social interaction, having a full schedule and places to invest your time, is invigorating."

Joining TheLadders was another part of Clark's strategy to keep his network up to date. "When I applied to a job on TheLadders, I often spoke to recruiters and HR people," he says. "I was able to add 20 to 30 people to my network that I kept in contact with."

Clark, who was looking for a position in new-business development that was director level or above, was also expanding his options in the working world. "My initial resume was focused on digital entertainment," he says. "But then, realizing it was getting tougher to get a job, I came up with two other resumes, one for platform sales and another for channel sales. I went in thinking I didn't need three resumes. I thought my network would come through. But as I had interviews and companies were not hiring, I realized this was a daunting task, and I needed a little more strategy to accomplish this."

Clark says he worked six to eight hours every day on his job search, contacting people in his network, crafting cover letters and doing volunteer work.

From media to technology

Clark received a good response to his resumes, but the economy wasn't cooperating. "I had final interviews with 10 or 12 companies over the past several months," Clark says. "I had a final interview with Warner Bros. the day they announced layoffs. They put the position I was interviewing for on hold. It was frustrating."

Frustrating, but not debilitating

He continued doing volunteer work, contacting his network and honing his cover letters. Eventually he heard from a recruiter with whom he had developed a good relationship after applying for a position he found on TheLadders. While that initial position didn't work out, the recruiter had another job that she thought would be a good fit. "She contacted me about a business-development role," he says. "It's technology based, and they needed a lot of the skills that I had. It's not content, but it's setting up client partnerships.

"The experience that I was going to be able to leverage was my ability to go out and deliver the core value proposition to clients and get them to sign up," Clark continued. "It was exactly what I had done in the past, just with different clients. Same process, same sales cycle, same methodology."

And, after going more than a year without a job, it took just one month from first interview to an offer to be the director of business development for Answer Financial, a division of White Mountains Insurance Group Ltd.

A yearlong search

While Clark was eager to take time off after his last position, he hadn't planned on taking such a long break. He says it's good to be working again. But he hasn't let all that he accomplished while he was looking for jobs fall by the wayside. "I'm still doing the committees. I can't spend as much time as I used to, but it's great; I love doing it. I feel more rounded."

Clark says if there's anything else he's learned, it's that during a job hunt it's easy to lose confidence in your abilities. "You need to be conscious of doing things to build confidence," he says. "Joining committees, sitting down with someone who needed help with a business plan, was a good thing for me. It's important to put yourself in situations where other people value what you say."

Otherwise, he says, it can be hard to go on interviews and convince other people you can offer them something of value. "You'll begin to wonder, 'What am I doing wrong? I must not be as smart as I thought.' It's not a good place to be.

"So, if you're unemployed, don't spend your time inside. Get out; talk to people, and find out how you can be of value. Being involved in my community is the silver lining to being unemployed. But it did take me a long time to see that silver lining."

> **"Volunteering, having a full schedule and places to invest your time, is invigorating."**

Job Fairs Reach the Senior Ranks

"JOB FAIR" SOUNDS like such a quaint term. Nostalgic, but that's only good if you remember coming away from one with an internship or entry-level gig that would impress your buds on campus. Mid-career, with a few jobs behind you and a justifiable need for the kind of salary that doesn't show up at "job fairs" too often, the whole thing seems more pointless than nostalgic.

But the job-fair concept is moving upstream. Seventy percent of recruiters polled by the Society for Human Research Management say they attend career fairs. Furthermore, the economy is pushing organizations that operate those job fairs to include jobs more appropriate to mid- and senior-level executives. The events now serve much the same purpose as industry-association meetings and other good networking events.

Should you attend job fairs as part of your job-search plan? The answer is yes, but not for the reason you think. Don't expect to walk away from a job fair with a job or even a good recruiter contact. Instead, think of attending as an opportunity to network, polish your interview skills and dig for job leads.

"Think about it: You're going to a place filled with people with the same professional background, a lot of the same interests, all there to talk about the job market—who's hiring, who's laying people off, what companies are looking for different kind of skills. It's networking," says Irene Marshall, a certified resume writer, career coach and president of coaching service Tools For Transition. "Just being there reminds you that the way you're going to get your next job is through meeting people."

To make the most of the job-fair scene, choose the right events for you, and walk in prepared to walk away with the most that you can. Traditional job fairs are usually organized by local job-search clubs, volunteer groups, churches and other organizations to bring together job seekers and companies with openings. They vary according to both the jobs and those who might benefit the most from them. If it's a professional organization, generally it will have a substantial networking and job-seeking component to it, and the cost of joining or attending meetings will be low.

Alternatively, an event organized by a company whose goal is to help people find jobs might be very effective because it has vetted both the companies and the people attending to make sure they're at least in the same topic area. On the downside, they might be so focused on running the event as a business that they don't concentrate enough on making the matchups work, or on encouraging attendees to help each other.

Commercial career events tend to cost more than local job fairs, but they have to demonstrate that they're able to deliver either the information or the hiring companies before they're worth a job seeker's time or money. Events organized by local government agencies or chambers of commerce tend to be more scattershot, rounding up companies to participate only because they're local. In either case, recruiters agree that the best way to improve the odds is to make sure there's sig-

HOW TO TREAT VOLUNTEER ASSIGNMENTS ON YOUR RESUME

BESIDES presenting new opportunities in your job search, volunteer work can fill in the gaps on your resume.

When it comes to presenting volunteer work in writing, treat it like a job. Certified professional resume writers advise clients to handle an extended volunteer job on your resume as you would any other position, provided it is related to your profession and you can demonstrate what you accomplished at the charity.

It should be listed in your job history, with all the relevant information, but the entry should clearly state that it was a volunteer position.

nificant overlap between your skills, background and interest in getting a job with the organization that puts together the event.

The best reason to try job fairs or other events, though, is that they really are tailor-made for people looking for jobs. They're like mixers for people too shy to mix on their own. "It's a safe environment to go job-seeking," Marshall says. "Even if you're already employed, it's an acceptable way to research the job market. It's a good tool for meeting people, making contacts, learning what's going on."

Pick Your Party

THE FIRST THING TO REALIZE is that you have to be as picky about your events as you are about any other use of your time. And don't judge an event by the name or location of the group that is holding the event.

A well-regarded California publisher has invited Marshall to speak at its job fair/conference every year for the past five years, but in all that time she hasn't signed up a single client. And she got the feeling she hadn't helped the attendees much, either. The job seekers were too far down the salary ladder to be able to afford personal coaching, and they were at the wrong point in their careers to be able to use her best advice, she explains.

On the other end of the spectrum, Marshall attended a volunteer organization with few industry credentials but a lot of enthusiasm. The group not only packed the church function rooms where it was held, but it spilled over into the sanctuary and was thick with mid-career people helping each other out on job searches. The crowd was smartly broken into groups focused on specific industries or job functions. And Marshall liked the mix it attracted. "Their meetings are on Saturdays, so they draw people who are working as well as those who are unemployed."

Sometimes you have to make the leap and attend an event you might not be sure is going to be helpful, but most of the time you can do enough research to tell how useful it will be ahead of time. The more similar to your goals or specialties an organization is, the more likely it is that you'll find good contacts, good information or a good lead on a job there. Professional associations, conferences and trade shows are especially good for that.

> Show up early. Sit next to strangers. Everyone at a job fair will have been doing research in his or her own focus area and most will be willing to share their findings.

Do Your Research

YOU CAN'T WALK IN COLD. Be prepared ahead of time, and participate. "If you can speak at some of these conferences, that's even better," says Charlene Li, president of the Altimeter Group, a research firm. "Then you're the focal point, and you're the one giving the information. When you're networking, it's what you're giving, not necessarily what you're getting, that's important right then."

"If you're the speaker, you don't have to worry about chasing people down later," Marshall adds. "They follow up with you."

Just walking in and trying to talk or hand out a resume to everyone doesn't work. It takes too much time and effort, and it makes you look a little desperate. "You should know what companies you want to talk to before you get there; know what you want to ask them or what information you want to give them," Marshall says. "When you've done that, you have time to wander around and find things you didn't know about before."

Conference sessions where there are specific topics on the agenda are good venues because you know at least one set of interests of everyone who goes to that session. "Look at the agenda ahead of time, and if there's just one session you're interested in, see if they'll let you sign up for just that one. Get there early, scope out the place, sit in the right spot," Li advises. "Talk to the other people that are there early—they're not going to be there early if they're not interested in the topic. Find out what they know, who they know that you should talk to; find out who in the room is influential in that area and talk to them."

If it's a traditional job-fair format, don't stand by while someone else talks to the contact you want to make. Leave a business card; then come back when the subject of your interest is free. And talk—to everyone, not just the people behind the counters. Chat with people in line; chat with people at the bar. Show up early; sit next to strangers. Everyone at a job fair has been doing research and most will be willing to share their findings with you. That kind of information is the most valuable kind of intelligence for a job seeker.

EXECUTIVES' 11-STEP GUIDE TO JOB FAIRS

1. Avoid general/government job fairs.
Events organized by local government agencies and chambers of commerce tend to be unfocused, involving companies because they're local, not because they're relevant.

2. Target a session or recruiter, and get there early.
Look at the agenda ahead of time to see if there's a particular session, recruiter or company in which you are interested. Get there early and talk to other early arrivals; they probably have a special interest in the topic or company. Find out what they know and who they know you should talk to. Find out who in the room is influential in that area and talk to them.

3. Don't hover or wait in line.
Don't stand still while someone else talks to the contact you want to meet. Pick up the contact's information and leave your card; come back when the contact is free, or follow up later.

4. Research the host.
Before you attend, learn about the organization hosting the event. Check it out online. Find members or leaders in the group, and call or write them for details. Sometimes you have to make the leap and attend an event you aren't sure will be helpful, but most of the time you can do enough research to know before you go.

5. Match yourself to the host.
Do research about who's behind the event so you can identify the best match for your skills, background and interests. A pharmaceutical marketing manager in New Jersey will get more mileage out of an event hosted by an organization of New Jersey pharmaceutical marketing managers than by a general marketing-industry event.

6. Research the companies in attendance.
Read up on the companies going to the event; make a list of the ones you want to talk to and what you can glean from them. If you can narrow down the list to identify the actual company representative to whom you'd like to speak, you can prepare a better case for why you'd make a good contribution to his or her team.

7. Participate.
Find a way to be more than an attendee. If you're the speaker, you don't have to worry about chasing down recruiters or fellow job seekers. They will find you.

8. Be prepared.
Prep for a job fair, a professional conference or a meeting of a professional organization just as you would for a job interview, a presentation or a meeting with a client. You must demonstrate that you are knowledgeable, professional and capable.

9. Bring a resume.
Unlike the Internet, where most job applications occur these days, in-person events require a paper resume you can hand out. Follow the resume rules: no images, no fonts that can't be scanned.

10. Bring business cards.
You might also want a private business card. If you're still working and are uncomfortable handing out your work card, have some made up with your name and private contact info. They're cheap, they're easy to hand out, and they give the impression of professionalism.

11. Talk to everyone.
Talk to your fellow job seekers. Job fairs are tailor-made for people looking for jobs. Think of them as mixers. Everyone at a job fair has been doing their own homework, and most will be willing to compare notes with you.

CHECKLIST: NETWORKING

BE VISIBLE

The No. 1 rule of networking is to be visible in your element. Make sure people can find you and see you every day.

○ Have you updated your online social networks (Facebook, Twitter, LinkedIn) to represent your latest professional accomplishments or demonstrate your expertise on a significant issue in the minds of your peers?

○ Stay active in industry organizations. Do you participate in any professional organizations? Do you volunteer your time and offer your expertise to your peers in these organizations?

○ Did you seek out opportunities to participate in panel disussions, speak to an organization or be quoted as an industry expert in the media?

KEEP IN TOUCH

○ Have you called people this week to talk about shared professional interests?

MAKE NEW FRIENDS

○ Have you taken the opportunity to introduce yourself to new influencers in your industry?

DON'T BEG BUT DO BE PERSISTENT

○ Does your network know you are available for work and have you continued to promote yourself as an expert? This is a better strategy than asking for a job.

BE AN INFORMATION BROKER

○ Have you done your homework to stay abreast of the latest trends and issues affecting your industry?

○ Have you approached peers at companies facing those issues to ask about what they're facing and offered your own expertise on the matter?

○ Have you used your position as a connector to introduce people in your network who may be able to help each other?

TAKE ONLINE CONNECTIONS OFFLINE

○ Have you approached any members of your online social network to ask for an in-person meeting? By meeting people offline, you'll build a stronger network online, and vice versa.

DON'T FIND A PARTY, THROW A PARTY

○ Have you organized a group of peers who would be interested in discussing industry trends and helping to boost each others' careers? By being the group organizer, you're immediately positioned as a leader people will want to speak with and get to know.

YOUR "JOB-APPLICATION HOTLINE"

○ You see a job you want in a target company. Have you prepared a list of contacts you can turn to for insights and introductions?

RECONNECT WITH MENTORS

○ Name five people you would regard as role models in your own career. What are they up to now and when did you last speak with them?

1._____

2._____

3._____

4._____

5._____

NEVER APOLOGIZE

BEATING INTERVIEW STAGE FRIGHT

INTERVIEW

FROM THE MOMENT YOU WALK IN, BE REAL

HAVE GOOD C

PREPARE TO OVERCOME OBJECTION

THE ELEVATOR PITCH

COMFORT WITH YOUR COSTUME

INTERVIEW LIKE AN ACTOR

ASK QUESTIONS; DON'T FREEZE

PICK THREE TALKING POINTS

R-

BRUSH UP

WING

UESTIONS

HANDLING AGE AND SALARY

GETTING PREPPED

Boy, did I bomb that job interview, and I was feeling really down. I was coming out of business school and had scored an interview with a top investment firm. I'd had a few great rounds with the team, but that day I was meeting with the "name" partners.

The senior partner was, frankly speaking, not my cup of tea. I just wasn't clicking with this guy, and then he dropped my least-favorite interview question of all time. It's the question that they teach you not to ask in Interviewing 101 because it is so obvious and so easily manipulated by the interviewee. "What's your greatest weakness?"

"Brevity."

And, not saying another word, I stared politely right back at him. Probably with a little bit of a wise-ass grin. OK, it was a pretty juvenile response, and I let my capricious side get the better of me.

Needless to say, things went downhill from there, and the interview ended in a polite, "don't-let-the-door-hit-you-on-the-way-out" manner a few minutes later. And I felt like a schmuck.

It's inevitable that, some days, in some places, you'll really goof up an interview. A job interview is artificial and awkward. You can feel like a butterfly under the magnifying glass, and it is uncomfortable to have somebody else poking and prodding you. It's how we handle the recovery that makes us great professionals.

The best way of overcoming the failed job interview is to show those people who witnessed your setback that you are made of sterner stuff. Write polite but brief thank-you notes, and be gracious. There's no sense whatsoever in trying to overcome your gaffe, so don't address it. You'll feel like you've come out a little bit ahead, and your interviewers will feel like your show of class is impressive.

And a brief word to the wise: You really need to separate your emotions from your rational assessment of your performance. I can't tell you how many hires we've made at TheLadders who later confided to me that they thought they had done poorly in the interviews. It is natural to feel anxious about the interview, but don't let that fool you into thinking you've actually, really and truly blown it.

Finally, learn from the experience. What was it that tripped you up? Knowledge about the company? Insight into that new technology? A few questions about an area that you hadn't really thought about in the past few years? Whatever it was, use this as an opportunity to bone up for future interviews. Never see failure as failure—it's just a chance to get better for the next time.

Get Prepped

THE JOB INTERVIEW IS AN UNUSUAL SITUATION: You're put in a room you've never been in, with a person you've never met, to talk about a company you don't work at, in order to persuade somebody that you'll be excellent at a job you don't have. No wonder it feels artificial. However, there are ways to make your job interviews both less nerve-racking and more effective.

First, pick three points and stick to them. Ever watched the politicians on TV? When the host asks them a real zinger of a question, you'll notice they rarely get flustered. Instead, they reply right off the top of their heads with an answer that seems to be completely coherent and well-crafted. In this chapter, we'll show you how to stay "on message" no matter what questions you're asked.

Second (and this may be surprising), the interview is not about you. If you think about it from your future boss' point of view, the interview is about how well you fit into his or her needs. If you stick to your talking points, you'll avoid one of the most common errors people make in job interviews: talking about themselves without a real purpose.

And last, have good questions. Even though Marc is usually the final person to meet a candidate at TheLadders, he is always surprised when people he's interviewing say they don't have any questions for him. Sure, you've already met four of his colleagues and they've answered a lot of the open questions you had about TheLadders, but, really? You have absolutely no good questions for the CEO?

Asking questions is only 50 percent about addressing your needs, explaining the role to you and satisfying your curiosity. The other 50 percent is showing your capability to think critically about the company, the industry and the role. In the pages that follow you'll find a list of questions we love to hear. Use that time to show off your good noodle by asking (brief) insightful questions.

Pick Three Talking Points

NO MATTER WHAT THE QUESTION IS, and no matter how impertinently put, the politician has an answer and doesn't get distracted by the host's badgering. We can't say whether that's good for us voters, but we *can* tell you it's deadly effective for giving a great interview.

It's called "staying on message," and the politicians don't do it by accident.

Before they go on TV, they write down (or have written down for them) talking points that make the key arguments they want to make. And whatever else happens, they make sure to get their talking points across.

So in order to ace your interviews, you'll want to have your own talking points. And here's the truly amazing thing—you don't even need to come up with them on your own. Unlike the fickle electorate, your target audience will tell you exactly what you need to say! All you have to do is ask them.

When you are setting up the interview, ask the recruiter or HR person: What are the three key things you're looking for in this position? And why are they important to the company? (If you're not able to get this question in beforehand, you can still ask it right at the start of the interview.)

They might say this position is for a new initiative, or this role is critical for the implementation of a company strategy, or the boss needs an expert to help assist in this area.

Whatever the three key needs for the role are, write down beforehand how you can fill those needs. Don't over-practice, just make sure that you know their three needs by heart and you've got a reasonable argument for why you can help them.

Then, during the interview, if conversation veers to upcoming spring training or the snow this winter, you just make sure that you steer it back to how you can contribute on the three key needs.

Stay on message, and when you walk out, your message will stay behind with your future boss.

Remember, It's Not About You

OF COURSE, DURING AN INTERVIEW you need to discuss your career goals, but only in the context of how they match up with what your boss is looking for. And yes, you need to discuss your prior performance and successes, but only to the extent that it supports how you match the three key needs the company has for the open position.

A job interview is a sales call—it's about selling you, your experiences, skills and talent for the role. It's not an A&E biography about you; it's a discussion about the company, its needs, the role, and how well you do, or don't, fit into the company's plans.

And it is most especially not a chance for you to get distracted by extraneous topics that may be very important to you but have absolutely nothing to do with how well you can do the job. Because the following topics are *very* important to you and you've been thinking about them a lot, you'll need to make an extra-special effort to avoid dwelling on them in the interview:

• How difficult the job search is. (OK, yes it is, but how is talking about this going to help you shorten your job search?)

• What your perfect career would be. (We're not here to talk about your perfect career, we're here to talk about this job and who we should hire for it.)

• The wrong decisions made by your previous boss/company/colleagues. (How is this helping you get your next job? It's not. Avoid.)

If we can be slightly tongue-in-cheek, the rule for job interviews is: "He who talks the least, wins." If you can get your interviewer talking about their needs, their hopes, and their viewpoints, you'll be collecting a lot more information about what it takes to get the job. Making your key points can take as little as 10 minutes if you're strictly on message. Use the rest of your time to find out what else you need to know to make your case.

Have Good Questions

IT'S ESSENTIAL TO HAVE GOOD QUESTIONS READY—even if you're meeting the nth person at the company you're interviewing with. Here are 10 questions that are good for almost any interview, plus a bonus question that will really make you stand out:

1. What's the biggest change your group has gone through in the last year?
2. One year from now, if I get the job, what will earn me a "gold star"? What are the key accomplishments you'd like to see in this role over the next year?
3. What's your (or my future boss's) leadership style?
4. About which competitor are you most worried?
5. How do your sales/marketing/technology/operations work here?
6. What kind of people are successful here? What kind of people are not?
7. What's one thing that's key to your success that somebody from outside the company wouldn't know about?
8. How did you get your start in this industry? Why do you stay?
9. What are your best and worst working relationships with other groups in the company?
10. What keeps you up at night? What's your biggest worry?

And here's the bonus, our favorite, and the best way to really demonstrate how much value you're going to add to your boss's career:

> How do you (Mr. or Ms. Future Boss) get a gold star/big bonus/your boss's recognition and thanks at the end of the year? How can I best help you do that?

Why is this question so good? It shows you're thinking about others, not just yourself. It shows that you want to be helpful and help the boss and the team achieve.

And it gets your future boss thinking about how beneficial it is going to be to have somebody like you on the team helping to achieve their goals.

What Recruiters Think of Your Interview

IT TAKES A BRAVE SOUL to offer interviewing advice to C-level candidates; tell a top earner how to ace the interview and you're likely to get a rather glib response. "Thanks, but I've been doing this for 15 years. I think I have it down by now," a New York IT manager in the financial industry recently told us.

Most likely, it's not a lack of manners but a lack of patience. Top-level candidates are often resistant to being schooled in details they're certain they've mastered during their years of experience. "I manage a team of 20 people," the candidate continued. "Three of them manage four additional people each. I've interviewed more times than I can count on both hands. I don't need interview advice, I need the job!"

Not so fast, say the recruiters who set up these interviews: The road from landing an interview to being handed a job offer is paved with potholes that can trip up even the most seasoned candidates. "You don't need to be green or entry-level to make mistakes in your interview process," explains Greg Bennett, a recruiter at the Mergis Group in Cary, N.C.

It is always a surprise to hear that even candidates at the top of their game and the peak of their careers can still stumble on some of the basics—sometimes from sheer lack of practice. Cindy Schneider, a corporate recruiting consultant at Intuit in Fort Collins, Colo., warns that "often people who have been with a company for a long time have not interviewed in even longer."

In fact, even as the courting gets more intense and the job offers grow larger, recruiters will tell you that the basic tenets of good interviewing endure. "Interviewing at the six-figure level is really no different from interviewing at the entry level, because what is an interview? Nothing more than an exchange of information," explains Jim Brown, president of Jim Brown Associates in San Francisco.

A job interview is a sales call—it's about selling you and your experiences and skills and talent for the role.

Brush Up

THE FACT IS, UNLESS YOU'VE BEEN JOB-HOPPING every two years, your interviewing skills are probably out of practice. This isn't something to feel down about but a good thing: a sign that you've made a long-term, dedicated effort at fewer companies. Rather than being an expert job hunter, you're an expert in your field.

Nevertheless, you'll want to brush up on your interview skills before you get there.

"Candidates sometimes forget certain skills," says a Chicago-based recruiter. "I remind them not to interrupt, don't tap your pen on the desk, don't insert the person's name into your answers and don't hang yourself—if you're asked what time it is, don't tell them how to build a watch. Common-sense stuff, but it gets forgotten."

You'll probably want to tune your elevator pitch as well. What will you say when you have 30 seconds to sell your merits to a stranger? Prepare your pitch. "You should know how you're going to tell them who you are. You should be practicing saying what you want to say before an interview, even at the senior level," advises Bennett.

Do Your Research, Come Prepared

MORE THAN ONE RECRUITER EXPRESSED SURPRISE that seasoned professionals still walk into interviews without conducting basic research on the company where they were hoping to land a high-paying job—especially with the information more readily accessible than ever before. "A candidate should have some knowledge about the company where they are interviewing," warns Harold Laslo, a staffing specialist at the Aldan Troy Group in New York.

"To walk in totally unprepared at a senior level is very harmful when you could have gone to their Web site and gotten a minimal amount of background information about them." Candidates who don't even show this base level of initiative are unintentionally telling the company that they're not the best person for the job.

Frank Laux, president of Strategic Search Partners in Keller, Texas, suggests that candidates bring printouts of their research from the company's Web site to the interview, just in case they need it. "Bring relevant information to demonstrate your qualifications, including past awards, letters, ad copy, portfolio material and so on. Bring extra copies of your resume. Have a legal pad or portfolio with you to take notes with a high-quality pen," says Laux.

Part of being prepared is understanding what kind of interview you're on and what your interviewer is really looking for that day. "A lot of times, in an initial interview they're just looking to see if you fit in, if you will all get along. It might be different from the drilling down you'd be doing if you were talking to the person who will end up being your boss," Brown adds.

Be Humble

IN YOUR CURRENT JOB, YOU MIGHT BE KING OF THE HILL. Few people will interrupt you when you speak, nobody will think less of you for boasting about your accomplishments, and you'll be forgiven if you veer into territory unrelated to the business at hand. It's for exactly this reason, recruiters say, that even the most successful job candidates can forget to tone it down when they walk into an interview.

"The key thing candidates should do is not talk too much. Listen to the questions asked, and answer them as succinctly as possible," Brown says. If you do brag—after all, you're there to sell yourself—make sure it's about the right thing.

"Very often [candidates are] more interested in tooting their horn or beating their chest and regaling the interviewer with their accomplishments in regards to the positions that they're going for, when they may not relate to the role at hand," Laslo says.

Show Genuine Interest

NO MATTER HOW HARD the interviewing firm is courting you and no matter how many "deal sweeteners" they've showered upon you, keep in mind that you still have to prove them right before you get an offer. Art Romero, managing director of Academy Recruiting in Denver, says that when he deals with executives, especially in the finance world where he does most of his recruiting, "there are a lot of big egos.

"One mistake is that when candidates get to the final interview—which is often just a formality—they assume the job is already theirs. Instead of asking about perks, they're joking about the accommodations they were put up in. By not fighting for the job, they don't get it," Romero says. Candidates who ask about what's next or when they can be promoted further before they've even landed the job can be seen as not showing the appropriate level of interest in the job at hand.

Beating Interview Stage Fright

"SOMETIMES NERVES TAKE OVER AND YOU DON'T SHOW WHO YOU ARE."

Those are the words of an auditioning actor in "Every Little Step," a documentary that follows the process of casting the 2006 Broadway revival of "A Chorus Line." But they could just as easily have been spoken by anyone who has ever been nervous before a job interview or looked back on his interview performance with regret.

Whether you are an actor stepping onto an audition stage or a job seeker entering a conference room, the pressure to deliver to the best of your ability can cause anxiety that threatens to cripple your performance.

For some job seekers, nerves can be disabling. Something happens when they walk through the door of the interviewer's office. Cold sweat trickles down the backs of their knees. Their minds draw a blank when asked basic questions like, "Where do you see yourself in 10 years' time?" or, "Why would you like to work for this company above all others?" These candidates feel like they're back at school in front of a crowded assembly, unable to make those words pass their lips.

Actors call it stage fright—the fear of underperforming in front of a paying audience or at an audition—and almost all good actors acknowledge battling it at one time or another. Many learned tricks early on to overcome a paralyzing phobia that can kill their careers.

Interview Like an Actor

THERE ARE MANY THINGS that job interviewees can do to stave off stage fright. For actor John Treacy Egan, star of such Broadway hits as "The Producers" and "The Little Mermaid," the key to overcoming nerves and ensuring you ace the audition is simple: preparation.

"I really need to be prepared," he says of going on auditions. "You sometimes think, 'Oh, I will do fine, and it will get me to the next stage.' You can get lax like that as an actor. You really need to give that performance the first time and not rely on a callback. Be as prepared as you can be."

Jodie Bentley, owner and co-founder of The Savvy Actor, a New York firm that coaches actors on the business of acting and teaches them how to market themselves, supports Egan's philosophy that preparation is vital. "So many people just wing it and say, 'I am just going to be me!' And then when we get in the interview situation, we all clam up if we don't have something planned and prepared."

Comfort With Your Costume

WHAT YOU WEAR FOR YOUR INTERVIEW or audition can set the stage for your nerves: It can sap your spirit or boost your confidence. "I'm coaching an actress who is really a leading lady, but she is having trouble owning [those roles]," Bentley says. "You need to dress that part, and that confidence will come. I think [the right clothing] helps body language in an interview as well."

Your appearance extends to all aspects of your physical presentation—your posture, pose, expressions and voice. "Always try to put yourself in comfortable situations," Egan says. "You have a lot of people around you in the professional world to help you. Ask them, 'Does my outfit look correct? Does my voice sound right? Is my hair cut right?' Practice interviews with your friends."

FAVORITE QUESTIONS ASKED BY RECRUITERS

"What is the best way for me to represent you to hiring managers?" In other words—and I am not being facetious, so this is no time to be modest—what makes you so good?
— *Ed Sordellini, executive recruiter in Wilmington, N.C.*

"Why should we hire you versus someone with equal skills and background?" This question gives you the opportunity to sell yourself in the proper context, to expand upon your skills and abilities without gloating. When answered well, it can be a true difference-maker.
— *Harold Laslo, a staffing specialist at the Aldan Troy Group in New York*

"What other types of jobs are you currently considering?" You don't need to reveal too much. However, if you are negotiating with another firm, you can say that you are looking at another opportunity but at this point are very interested in moving forward with this position.
— *Frank Laux, president of Strategic Search Partners in Keller, Texas*

"How do you plan to keep up with the industry?" Discuss the news articles, industry journals, books, Internet and other resources you use to stay up-to-date. You can mention examples of certifications you have earned, continuing education, industry awards and so on.
— *Frank Laux*

I ask hiring managers, "What's that hot button or mystery meat you're looking for? What is it about a candidate that's going to get you to reach across the desk, grab them by the tie, and say, 'You've got to work here!' "
— *Greg Bennett, recruiter at the Mergis Group in Cary, N.C.*

"What is your claim to fame? What makes you special? Why would a company want to hire you?" It forces you to be creative when you think of an answer, to think on your feet. Be prepared for it.
— *Greg Bennett*

"Why are you interested in becoming a _____, working for _____, or leaving your company to join this one as a _____?" In other words, what is it about this particular position that has you interested in it?
— *Art Romero, managing director of Academy Recruiting in Denver*

I am going to want to know why you are leaving your current job, so you should be ready with an answer.
— *Art Romero*

Look out for "Oh, and just one more question ..." This is usually the most important one. Here's your parting shot. Make sure you catch it.
— *Art Romero*

What if you are well dressed, well groomed and well prepared, but you still feel like a panic attack is approaching? Stage fright, says Egan, usually occurs about five minutes before the actor goes on stage. Actors neutralize the paranoia by breathing, he says. "Whenever you start to experience fear, the first thing that you have to do is remember to breathe. Fear stops your breathing and everything starts to tighten. Breathing opens the door to relaxation."

Bentley recommends a breathing exercise that she does before going on stage or before a big meeting or audition: "It is rapid breathing through the nose. It really centers you and calms you."

Egan advises that you give yourself a chance to shake it off. Literally. "Shake your limbs and jump up and down and give the adrenalin the chance to have an outlet of actual movement." If you're feeling the pains of panic set in, find yourself a private space—a lobby bathroom or a secluded corridor—and practice these breathing and shaking tips to beat back stage fright.

The Elevator Pitch

BENTLEY INSTRUCTS HER CLIENTS to practice role-playing exercises before an audition and to have an elevator pitch or monologue memorized and at the ready. Everyone's interview routine should include a 30-second blurb, she says. "If someone says, 'Tell me about yourself,' you already have a monologue or blurb ready to go." She encourages her clients to rehearse their elevator pitch and asks that it convey "something personal about you, showcase your strengths and show what you are passionate about."

Bentley believes the elevator pitch should be carefully crafted and learned. "Type it out. Say it to yourself in the mirror. Look at yourself while you are doing it."

Also, research all you need to know about the company where you hope to work. Prepare your thoughts about the business and industry and have some ready answers about them, Bentley advises.

From the Moment You Walk In, Be Real

THE INTERVIEW ISN'T JUST HOW YOU ANSWER QUESTIONS or explain your skills, Egan says. That would be like limiting an actor's audition to his reading and singing. "From the moment you walk through the door, you have to be available as a real person. You cannot shut down when you aren't singing and dancing. You want to be present for all of it. It is the same for an interview. You take yourself on as a character."

Bentley warns her clients about being overly intimidated and losing the essence of their personalities in the process. "Many people get into interview settings and look at that person across the table as an authority figure. I think that is the worst thing that you can do."

Bentley encourages interviewees to show their passions and interests because people want to work with people they like. "That is definitely a rule in theater. If a director is going to be working with you for four to eight weeks straight, he has got to like you first. And it is the same if somebody is going to bring you onto a team in their company: They need to like [the person] they are going to be working with. People want to work with people who are passionate."

The Multiple-Person Interview

IN A ONE-ON-ONE INTERVIEW, you can balance your energy against that of the other person. "You can sense the temperature in the room much quicker in a one-on-one than with a group," Egan notes. If the interview is with a group of interrogators, your balance and attention are taxed like an actor on stage connecting to an audience.

The first rule: Acknowledge everybody in the room.

Bentley agrees. "When you have a room full of people," she says, "your job is to keep the energy up in the air a little bit more. It is more of a hot-seat situation. You need to take in the whole room and not just answer one person. Eye contact is really important."

Ask Questions; Don't Freeze

CONFIDENCE IN THE INTERVIEW or audition is evident when you are fully prepared. "I would recommend preparing stories about your resume that show your personality, your strengths or your work ethic," Bentley advises. "If you have these prepared and memorized to a certain degree, you will always have something that you can pull out of your back pocket if the nerves begin to take over."

Egan suggests notecards as a last resort. "Even if you have to look down, at least you're getting your point across as opposed to freezing."

Another way to keep grounded and in the moment it is to have a few questions prepared to ask the interviewer. "If you get stuck and you don't know what else to say, don't just sit there. Have a couple of questions prepared and know your audience," Bentley says. She instructs her clients to have three personal questions and three business questions prepared that they can insert at any moment. "So if you know that a person lives in a certain area of the town, you could ask if they have ever gone to a particular pizza parlor. Or if you know that they went to a certain college and you know someone that went there, you can bring that up."

"Always ask questions," Egan says. "An interested person is an interesting person." Take your time when you speak, and select your words. "Don't talk too fast. Speak clearly and slowly," he says.

Never Apologize

THE INTERVIEW IS UNDER WAY AND YOU STILL FEEL INSECURE. How can you project something you're not feeling? "Act it," Egan says. "You really have to fake it. No one will know. You have to tell yourself to be confident. It really is about pro-

10 BODY-LANGUAGE TIPS FOR THE INTERVIEW

Broadway actor John Treacy Egan and acting coach Jodie Bentley share advice on poses, positions and props.

1. Why your wardrobe matters
Wear clothes that show you in your best light. If you wear something that makes you feel great, your body language is going to be much more comfortable in the moment.

2. Hold onto a talisman
"A piece of jewelry or a scarf or something that has meaning to you can ground you in the moment," Bentley says. Looking down at your wedding ring, for instance, can remind you of the bigger picture, and why you really want the job.

3. Sit pretty
Keep both feet on the floor and sit up straight. Crossing your legs portrays complacency. Sitting a little bit forward on your chair will keep you composed. Leaning backwards can leave the impression that you are overly relaxed.

4. Steady those flying limbs
Nerves often cause people to cross their legs over and over, but nervous energy is not what you want to project. If you have to make a point, use your hands. But rest them on your knees until you need to make a gesture.

5. Don't fold your arms
Crossed arms close you off from the interviewer. An old actor's audition tip: Don't do it.

6. Tame your tics
Don't crack your finger joints, fiddle with your cufflinks or twirl your curls. Be aware of what habits you have when you're nervous and consciously avoid them.

7. No hands in pockets
"If you are standing at all, hands in the pockets are a big no-no. It just looks clumsy and messy," Bentley says. "Let your hands drop to your sides, and talk," is Egan's advice.

8. Keep your distance
"Some people just get too close for comfort," Bentley says. "They think that they want to make a connection, so they get closer. Respecting that boundary is really important." For example, don't stretch your hands or body over the interviewer's desk.

9. Use props
"If you need a prop like a pen, use it if it makes you feel more comfortable," Egan says. "But give yourself the chance to step away from that during the presentation or interview. It makes you look stronger."

10. Don't stare
"Actors never fully lock eyes with people," Bentley says. "We talk, we look people in the eyes, we have a thought, and we look away. If we start really staring at them and staying focused so much, we start to look a little crazy." If you feel like you are looking the person in the eye too long, hold it one more second and break away.

jecting confidence because nobody wants to hire somebody who is not confident."

A lot of actors walk into an audition and apologize for not being ready because they only received the music that day. Directors don't want to know that. "Don't apologize," says Egan. "Walk in and show them that you can carry the show. I hate to say this because it can be taken another way, but you are doing them a favor by being there. They need somebody to fill their position, and you are going to be really good at it."

Analyzing the Performance Afterward

"DON'T JUDGE THE INTERVIEW UNTIL IT IS OVER," Egan advises. "Oftentimes, you can go into an audition and feel you got the job, but you may never get the phone call. And if you feel like you did blow an opportunity, you should take a moment to learn from it and build upon it rather than repeat it."

It's always a good idea to give yourself a breather after an interview. Take the rest of the day (or week) off, then look back. Take credit for what went right, and redouble your efforts for next time on what to improve.

Handling Age and Salary

AGE DISCRIMINATION IS NEITHER LEGAL NOR FAIR. Nevertheless, it is prevalent in a variety of forms, and you need to be ready to confront it in an interview setting. Age discrimination isn't overt; it's more a function of who does the initial filtering of resumes and job candidates and the likelihood that those relatively junior staffers don't understand the real requirements of the job they're filling or what an experienced executive would bring to it.

"I found age discrimination pretty prevalent," says John B., 59, who was hired by a leading medical-equipment company six months after he was laid off from another job. "It wasn't overwhelming, but it was disheartening. You talk to a lot of recruiters who weed you out before you get to the manager to explain the value you can bring," says John. "And there are two parts to it: age, certainly, in my case, but with 28 years of experience, [it was also my] comp package."

It's almost impossible for job candidates to tell whether they're being judged or passed over based on their age or their salary. The sticking point could be just that the interviewer is surprised to see gray hair on a candidate she assumed was younger. "If you're an executive in your mid-50s who made it through the first screenings because you didn't put your first couple of jobs on your resume or excluded the year you graduated, you could walk into that interview and be talking to an HR person who's the age of your child," says Sally Haver of The Ayers Group/ Career Partners International.

Those relatively inexperienced screeners have usually been told that their responsibility is to say "no" as often and as quickly as possible to candidates who don't fit the pattern, according to Jim Villwock, founder of Job Doctors International.

"You're at the mercy of low-level people with a slate of profiles to match," he says. "You can address that by talking about the value you bring, but you have to be at the top of your game to do it. The subject matter you're presenting is difficult for people at that level."

The goal, Haver says, is to satisfy the interviewer that your qualifications fit the profile and that there are no other issues—such as age, health problems or unusually high salary requirements—that would disqualify you. "You want to convince them you're pass-on-able. If you are in this screening interview with HR, you want it to be as transparent as possible," she says.

Prepare to Overcome Objections

THE KEY TO BEING SUCCESSFUL ISN'T HIDING YOUR AGE OR SALARY but being prepared with explanations or propositions designed to overcome the objections that screeners of different types will bring up, according to Cheryl Palmer.

"Think like a salesperson, even if you're not," suggests Palmer. "A salesperson practices to deal with any objections you might bring up because they know what the potential objections will be." For a screener, it might be enough to demonstrate that you're still energetic, focused and vital.

Questions about compensation and authority are stickier but can be dealt with a lot more directly with the hiring manager than issues as legally dicey as age. "If you're talking to the hiring manager, you can cut to the chase and say, 'I can do everything you need done and more, and you're going to be thrilled,'" Haver says. "'You will not find anybody who can do this job better than I can do it, so let's talk about how you can bring me on board in a way that's comfortable for you.'"

Tough Interview Situations

EVERY CAREER GUIDE EVER WRITTEN covers the "tough" job-interview questions: Why do you want to work here? What is your greatest weakness?

That advice rarely extends to questions that cut closer to home: explaining away the DWI you got on the way back from dinner with a client or the rumors of fraud that painted everyone laid off from the finance department where you worked after the stock price collapsed. There is little to prepare you to answer questions about the well-respected boss who never got along with you and asked you to resign or the sexual-harassment charge leveled against you but dismissed years earlier.

It is not uncommon to have something lurking in your past or left off your resume that might upset your job search or present an obstacle in an interview. And it needn't be an Enron-scale scandal to cause you concern. A black mark on your record (like a negative statement in an employment background check or a lie uncovered in an employment and education verification check) can be enough to send a hiring manager on to the next candidate.

Recruiters and investigators who conduct employment background checks advise job seekers to know what their records will say to a potential employer and be prepared to correct or explain them in an interview.

"If they got a degree at a diploma mill, that will be revealed in a respectable background check; if they didn't work at an employer they listed, or didn't have the job title they say they had, that will come out," according to Les Rosen, former California deputy district attorney; president of Employment Screening Resources of Novato, Calif.; and founding member of the National Association of Professional Background Screeners.

The problem for job seekers is that there isn't a lot they can do to keep "secrets" under wraps while they're job-searching or even afterward. If you have a black mark on your record, expect it to surface, Rosen says. "When a person with something minor in their background tries to hide it, they are taking a risk."

"Almost everyone is doing background checks on every hire; it's the quickest way to get rid of applicants," says Jo Prabhu, founder and CEO of placement firm 1800Jobquest of Long Beach, Calif., and an expert on using background checks in hiring. "It goes even down to the administrative level; someone might be a felon or have some arrests. So they check everyone."

What Records Matter?

MOST EMPLOYERS AREN'T INTERESTED IN YOUR CRIMINAL PAST unless it's relevant to the job for which you're applying, according to Prabhu. Employers usually just want to know that you've done the time or paid the fine—essentially that things were made right and that the whole thing was resolved at least two years ago, she says.

"I did have a woman who got a DUI on New Year's Eve, but that was easy to explain," Prabhu says. "If it was something in college or not related to the job, employers aren't interested.

"If you're applying for a financial position, they'll do an additional credit check, and that might be relevant," she explains. "But they don't check civil suits or other things. It's too expensive, and it's not relevant."

"If during the last five years you were convicted of check fraud and I was hiring you to do a job where you had access to finances, that would be a concern," says Robert E. Capwell, chief knowledge officer at Employment Background Investigations Inc. of Owings Mills, Md. "If you were a registered sex offender and were working with children or with members of the opposite sex, that would be, too. The question is how long ago was the crime and how relevant is it to the job you're discussing."

Potential employers want to gauge their own level of risk or—more perversely, if your black mark involves the kind of financial shenanigans that made Wall Streeters rich at the expense of regulations and their own stockholders—whether you're still willing to play hardball.

"We'll find out pretty quickly if you say you were the vice president of operations

INTERVIEW PREP BY INDUSTRY

OPERATIONS

Operations professionals need to be able to show their value in an interview. This is the one tip recruiters who specialize in placing operations professionals keep coming back to.

"You have to show that your role has impacted the business in a broader scope. The most successful candidates understand the full scheme of things; your ability to communicate this is critical," says Ronald Parks, managing director at eConsult America in Minneapolis.

Furthermore, few interviewers are going to let you off with general responses.

"I want to know if they're

qualified," says Laux, "and I am going to ask them specifics, like what kind of cost-reduction work they have done, their spend level responsibility, and how they achieved these results."

A job candidate, especially a more established one, should expect to be asked what commodities they are (or were) in charge of and how big their fiduciary responsibility is. Give specific examples of how you have reduced costs and improved productivity.

SALES AND MARKETING

If you work in sales or marketing, odds are good that you're not worrying up a storm the night before a big job interview. Selling your skills and experience to

a new company? Figuring out what they're looking for? That's your thing. You've got it down.

"Sales people tend to have more control over their own destiny," says Romero. "If you're a good sales person and you generate revenue, it's hard to ignore your value."

But this doesn't mean that even the best sales and marketing gurus don't make mistakes in interviews. Recruiters have seen it all. They warn that, quite often, the sales and marketing resumes aren't optimized.

"If you're in sales and you're not screaming about how successful you were, you probably weren't beating the odds. What it should say is how much you sold and to whom and how much

[for an entire company] but it was only a department, and by verifying dates of employment, we'll find out if you say you worked somewhere for a year but it was only six months and you got fired and then didn't work anywhere for six months," Capwell says. "Former employers can't say much, but they are supposed to verify dates and titles."

Full Disclosure

ABOUT THE ONLY REAL SOLUTION TO A GLITCH in an otherwise resume-polished background is full disclosure, investigators and recruiters agree.

"Derogatory information honestly revealed and discussed by the applicant is much less harmful than if it's discovered by a third party," Rosen says. "Even if the company's not really looking, one of the most productive sources of background checks is co-workers.

your percentage exceeded the quota," says Bennett. "And you shouldn't lead off with your education; it's irrelevant to sales. I have got to know that you know how to sell."

Sales and marketing folks are generally good at reading and persuading others. In fact, Brown says that he's gotten feedback that some of his candidates were almost too charming—and talked too much.

"I tell them, 'You've got two ears and one mouth, so you should listen twice as much as you talk. Answer the questions that are asked of you, and don't go overboard,' " says Brown.

Finally, it would seem unusual to remind someone in sales of their ABCs (Always Be Closing), but sometimes even the most marketable candidates forget. "You gotta remember, if you're interviewing for a sales job, that you 'ask for the order.' Close the deal!" Brown says.

TECHNOLOGY

Though the old stereotype of a socially awkward, poorly dressed techie no longer dominates, recruiters say that even at the six-figure level, residual effects remain.

Speaking in "tech-ese," or using too many technical terms in an interview with people who may not share their background, is a common recruiter concern for candidates in search of tech-nology jobs.

You may know your stuff but need guidance on interpersonal skills. "Even with cutting-edge technology skills, [these candi-dates] still need to learn to speak in plain English to non-techies," says Laslo.

In a field where staying on top of the latest technology changes and developments is essential, Laslo says that he will always ask candidates how they plan to stay up-to-date.

"They may have skills with a technology that reached its peak two, three or four years ago, but a candidate can be left behind if they haven't adapted their skills since then."

HIRED! "DON'T SETTLE" WORKS FOR MANUFACTURING VP

 In what turned out to be a 12-month search for a new job, John B. did a lot to make things more difficult for himself.

He didn't lower his sights from the vice-president level he lost and wanted to regain; he didn't go along with the advice that he lower his expectations and salary requirements; and he didn't cut anyone any slack when it became apparent his age could be an issue.

"In phone interviews, people are certainly trying to judge your personality by listening to your voice," John recalls, "but they ask you key questions and try to disqualify you that way. Like, 'So ... tell me, what year did you get your MBA?' My question was, 'What's the relevance?' "

WHEN TO REVEAL WHAT

Graduation year could be relevant for a school that was going through a particular management philosophy at the time, acknowledges John, 59, who got his at the beginning of the '80s.

"There were times when people would tell me I didn't put down a year on my form and they wanted me to do that before they'd talk to me, and I said, 'We should talk first.' You have to be nice, but there's a point where I get into an honesty thing. What do they want that I don't have, and what do I have that they don't value?" he says.

JOB LOSS AT AGE 59

John spent more than 28 years in operations. He specialized in supply-chain management: purchasing raw materials and managing vendors, shippers and inventory. John made sure the manufacturers he worked for had the parts they needed when they needed them, didn't pay too much for them, and didn't over-pay for having too many on hand at any one time.

His new job, which he successfully located through TheLadders, is as a vice president, overseeing supply-chain and materials management for a medical equipment manufacturer.

His last job effectively ended six months before he was actually laid off. The CEO, looking for fresh blood, laid off seven senior vice presidents in the space of a few weeks, including John's boss. "I could have taken a smaller job working in one of the divisions, but the reality was the people running those divisions wanted to pick their own people," he explains.

So he started his job search before he actually got his pink slip. The most amazing thing, aside from the unexpectedly negative reaction to his age, was the assumption on the part of friends, colleagues and recruiters that he would and should take a more junior position than the one he'd been doing.

"I looked at a lot of those jobs, manager and director level rather than vice-president level, and it was stuff I was doing 10 years ago," he says. "I didn't want to

do that. I'm in it for a career, not just to put in my 40 hours and go home. If a guy came to me at age 59 and says he'd be willing to take a job one or two levels below where he was, I'd think he was just trying to ride out his time until retirement. I didn't want to be that guy."

PERSISTENCE PAYS

He stuck to his guns, refusing one job that offered a VP title but $30,000 less per year than he'd been led to expect. He also watched a number of opportunities either evaporate, go to younger and less qualified executives, or devolve into something too junior for him to want.

The job he eventually—and happily—got was a position that required John to move 350 miles from San Jose, Calif., to Los Angeles. "I was willing to move," John explains. "A lot of people weren't, so that was one advantage."

Another was the clear presentation of the value he could offer, defined by showing where and how he'd been able to save money on the purchase, shipment and storage of components in his previous job.

"I'd spent a lot of time the previous four or five years developing cost-reduction roadmaps," he says. "Bringing that to the table allowed me to talk about the things I can do. That made for a very clear picture."

"If you're a six-figure person, you have to start with the assumption there are a lot of people working with you or under you who are interested and are going to look you up," he says. "They're ready to go on the Internet and see if you're a sex offender—because that information isn't hard for consumers to find—or what degrees you're claiming in your LinkedIn profile or other business connection, and whether you ever went there."

Since there's not any real way to conceal derogatory information, it's better to know what might be disclosed about you during a background check. Have a background check done on yourself to check that the information is accurate. If you find false information, you can try to correct the inaccuracies, but there is little you can do to hide negative but accurate items. The best advice is to be prepared to explain them, and you can't do that until you know what someone will find.

"There are a lot of people with things on their record that aren't discharged—like a DUI that someone got a long time ago and then moved to another state before the state sent them a notice saying to pay the fine," Rosen says. "That would show up on your record looking as if you fled the state, even if it's not true.

"There is a dramatic increase in the number of searches being done and the types of tools that are being used," he says. "There will almost always be a driving record, for example. It's an inexpensive record to get, and it turns up DUIs or drug incidents that can reveal alcohol or drug problems."

Honesty is about the only choice, especially when waffling about tough questions would raise enough red flags that a potential employer would either drop you or investigate further, according to Villwock. "What [hiring managers] want to know," he says, "is, 'Are you going to do the same thing to me?' "

Interviewing Anywhere, Any Time

THE BOILERPLATE JOB INTERVIEW is a thing of the past. Job interviews no longer rely on the old blueprint—a visit to a corner office to meet a stream of executives in business suits for a straight session of questions and answers. The standard office meeting is still part of the interview process, but executives now face rounds of interviews that are likely to involve varied settings and situations that test the candidate's mettle and temperament under different conditions.

An applicant for an executive position is likely to face an interview by phone or Web conference, an interview at a job fair or conference, at lunch or over cocktails, at an interview by a casual acquaintance who recommended them, or in a face-to-face with four senior executives in a committee-style interview.

Human-resources executives are relying more on interviews by phone and Web conference to reduce the costs associated with business travel and to accommodate hiring managers' busy schedules. Moreover, many interview situations (like a lunch or committee interview) are designed to test a candidate's act outside the one-on-one office setting and determine how she will perform in the real world. In fact, job interviews can occur at the spur of the moment or happen even without you knowing it. (Think of a chance meeting with a competitor at a conference or a school play.)

The questions and answers don't change much from situation to situation, but the candidate's behavior in each setting will determine her success. Understanding the most likely interview scenarios and the proper behavior for each will prepare you to deliver the best performance you can and will boost your confidence. What follows are the most common interview scenarios and our advice for putting your best foot forward.

Phone Interview

THE PHONE INTERVIEW arguably requires the least preparation. You don't have to agonize about your outfit, you can have notes about the company at your disposal, and you even have the ability to use the Web to perform additional research during the conversation. But that doesn't mean you should approach a phone interview carelessly.

Be passionate: Most companies use the phone interview as a preliminary screening, a low-intensity interview conducted by a junior human-resources staffer to gauge the candidate's abilities and interest before investing an executive's time in an in-person interview. But when distance is a factor, phone interviews can take the place of site visits, and they will be intense. Either way, "You want to convey passion and professionalism," says Deborah Brown-Volkman, a professional certified coach and the president of a career, life and mentor coaching company. "Answer the phone with lots of energy. For example: 'It's nice to meet with you today! I am really looking forward to our interview.'" Don't be afraid to emphasize that you really want a job for fear of sounding desperate, Brown-Volkman counsels. "Say that you are excited about the job, that you are a perfect fit for the job and that you really want this job."

Be on time: Be ready at the appointed interview time. "I have done plenty of phone interviews where I know I have just woken people up or where there have been all kinds of other things going on in the background. I would encourage full attention," says Kelly Dingee, a sourcing researcher and executive trainer for AIRS, an executive search firm in Fairfax, Va. Also consider technical issues that must be

EMPLOYMENT BACKGROUND CHECKS: KNOW YOUR RIGHTS

As a job seeker, what are the chances that potential employers will run background checks on you? Excellent. Ninety-six percent of human-resources professionals claim their organizations perform background checks on potential employees and new hires, according to a recent poll by the Society for Human Resources Management.

What are they looking for? One-third of U.S. employers now use credit checks to screen applicants, according to a survey by the *Los Angeles Times*. Others verify claims made on your resume and in the job interview. Some look at criminal records, news reports and even sex-offender status.

It's important to remember that background checks can't be done without your permission. Employers are required to inform job seekers that they intend to perform a background check and receive written permission from the job seeker, according to the Privacy Rights Clearinghouse, a nonprofit consumer-information and advocacy organization.

If an employer chooses not to hire an applicant because of information gleaned from a background check, they're required to notify the job seeker and provide the name of the company that prepared the report; the law includes a loophole for employers who run background checks themselves.

managed before the start time. "If you use a headset, make sure it is a good one and that you don't have any noise on the line. Readiness is key."

Eliminate distractions: "If you have a dog, you need to find a place for that dog to be for the half-hour or 45 minutes that you are doing the phone interview," Dingee says. "If you are unemployed and you are at home taking care of the kids, you need to schedule the phone interview when you can have quiet time—not so much because you don't want employers to have insight into your private life but more because you want to be on your game. The less distraction you have, the better."

Be ready: Having notes handy in front of you is useful, but Dingee advises candidates to read up on the company, review its Web site and have an understanding of the organization's priorities. "You need to reflect back on the interviewer (and the company) during the interview and make sure it is about them as much as it is about you. You want them to know that you are genuinely interested and you have done your research," she says. "Phone interviews are quick," Brown-Volkman notes. "I would make a list of three bullet points that you want to make. If you don't get them across during the interview, you can wrap up by thanking the interviewer and then ask to leave him or her with three points."

Web Interviews

AS THE TECHNOLOGY GROWS MORE UBIQUITOUS, companies often substitute telephone interviews with Webcam or Web-conference interviews. The phone interview is still more common, but some companies prefer the Webcam interview as a way to size up the candidate visually before going to the expense of setting up an in-person interview, says Frank Risalvato, founder of the recruiting firm IRES Inc., in Charlotte, N.C. For certain jobs where the candidate might be required to meet with customers, clients or members of the public, HR can use the Webcam to gauge the candidate's presentation skills. "I have got companies that specifically request that if a candidate does not have a Webcam on their laptop to go out and buy one, and they will happily reimburse you the $19," Risalvato explains. For a successful Webcam interview, here's how to present yourself in the best possible light.

WHAT AN EMPLOYER *CAN* CHECK

The Fair Credit Reporting Act sets a national standard for employers to follow when conducting a background check on an applicant or employee. Checks can include:

- Credit
- Criminal history
- Driving records
- Interviews with neighbors, friends and associates

Rehearse: "A dry run with a friend is critical for you to have an idea of what to do and where to look, as well as any potential hiccups," Dingee advises. "Do the dry run at the same time of day that you have the Skype [or other Web] interview scheduled. If you have it scheduled at 7 o'clock on Monday night, then I would do it 7 o'clock Sunday night." Make sure there is sufficient light and that there will be no unexpected interferences at that time. Risalvato advises candidates to check that everything is working shortly before the interview. He gives his clients the option to connect with him via Yahoo or Windows Live about 45 minutes to an hour before the interview to rehearse.

Be conscious of your space: Try to make sure your space is de-cluttered. "You need to chase all dogs or cats or whomever may be in your environment out," Dingee says. "Also, I would check out what is behind me because I don't want anything to divert attention. Too many pictures of my kids, artwork, junk or something random that really isn't appropriate should be moved. Risalvato agrees. "I had a case where the person was in an Internet café but there was a wastepaper basket with plastic sticking out in the back right-hand corner, which was very distracting."

Take note of angles and lighting: Make sure that you have angled your Webcam correctly so that the interviewer isn't staring at your chest instead of your face. Stay centered in the frame of the camera. "You do need to have enough lighting to be able to have eye contact," Risalvato says. "I generally coach the person to put my window right below his or her Web camera so that their eye is naturally going to look at me. It can be difficult for someone who's not familiar with working with this kind of media to train one's eye to look directly into the Webcam."

Committee Interview

WALKING INTO A CONFERENCE ROOM AND FIELDING QUESTIONS from several interviewers can be nerve-racking. Being well prepared and maintaining eye contact with all the members of the committee are two starting points. Here are some other ways that you can impress the panel during a multi-person interview.

Who's who?: "To prepare for the interview, you want to find out who is in the room," Brown-Volkman says. "Sometimes you have people from different disciplines—from finance, from marketing, from operations. You want to know something about them so that whenever you're asked a question you can tailor the answer to their background. You would, for example, answer the marketing guy with a more marketing bent."

Dingee agrees. "I am a source researcher. So when I interview, I do a background search on the people I am talking to. I want to see what their level of experience is. Professional networks can give you some idea of what they are affiliated with and certainly if they have any other associations. If you are an engineer and you are interviewing with an engineering manager who is very active with a certain engineering association, that will give you a point of reference during the interview."

Position yourself: You usually don't know if it is going to be a roundtable or set up as a panel with you exclusively under the spotlight. "You need to position yourself and make sure that you are comfortable," Dingee says, "because you want to be able to appear at ease even if you are nervous."

Deidre Henry, a television and film actress, knows something about auditioning. She advises job seekers and actors alike to seek out a familiar or sympathetic face. "A lot of times when I will walk into a room, there is someone who knows me or knows my work. So they are on my side already, and my immediate thing is to connect with them

WHAT AN EMPLOYER *CAN'T* CHECK

According to the Privacy Rights Clearinghouse, the following information is off-limits to employers conducting background checks:

- Bankruptcies after 10 years

- Civil suits, civil judgments and records of arrest, from date of entry, after seven years

- Paid tax liens after seven years

- Accounts placed for collection after seven years

- Any other negative information (except criminal convictions) after seven years

to bring a sense of who I am to the group."

Maintain eye contact with everyone: "Relate the answer to the person who asked the question but include everyone else through basic eye contact," says actor Douglas Dickerman. "Maybe the person on the far left has asked the question. You need to make sure that you turn your attention to him or her but then also make eye contact, answer the question and look at everybody else. But light back up on the person who actually asked it. Reflect back and make sure that you answered the question completely."

Be yourself, but adjust your energy: You might be tempted to play to your audience and tune your personality to the personalities in the room. Don't do it. "Although you have to appeal to several different personalities, I subscribe to the school of just being yourself," says recruiter Risalvato. "If you try anything other than being yourself, it is eventually going to come up that they were sold on a different person. Don't modify your behavior, but be cognizant of the fact that you are in an interview."

Be yourself, Brown-Volkman agrees, but kick up the energy level a notch. After all, you are the center of attention!

Lunch Interview

THE LET'S-DO-LUNCH INTERVIEW can be a minefield of potential problems. What type of restaurant would you choose if the selection is yours? What sort of food is best to order? Should you have a drink?

Selecting the venue: A candidate is rarely required to choose a dining option to meet for an interview. "But if you are picking the restaurant ... pick something that is middle of the road," suggests Dingee. "You don't want them to feel that they have just blown their whole expense account for the month, taking you out to lunch for this interview. But you also don't want to look too casual." Brown-Volkman suggests that you find out what type of food the interviewer likes and then pick a place you know and where the service is good. Visit the restaurant the day before and reserve a good table. Get there early. "I would let the host, waiter or waitress know that you are there for a job interview and that you need to make a good impression."

Yes to fish. No to spaghetti: Because you can expect to be doing more talking than eating, order something light. "You don't want to be the last one done because you have been answering all of the questions," Dingee advises. Use some common sense when ordering. Select something that is safe and not messy to eat. Keep it really simple and streamlined. You don't want to go with a marinara sauce if you are wearing a white shirt. Fish can easily be cut with a fork and is a preferable choice over spaghetti or rice or string beans. "I wouldn't get a salad because it is so messy," Brown-Volkman notes.

Avoid alcohol: "James Bond can pull off a dry martini, shaken, not stirred. Not you. Staying away from hard alcohol is a smart move," says Risalvato. "I wouldn't go anywhere near hard alcohol during an interview. I would want to be focused. I would stick with an iced tea or a soft drink." Brown-Volkman says that even if the interviewer orders an alcoholic drink, you are not encouraged to do the same. A single glass of wine could be the exception, says actress Henry. "I follow the person I am with. If they order a glass of wine, I will order one glass, but if they were to order a strong drink, I just wouldn't." You know yourself best, but remember you are the one in the hot seat and you want all your wits about about you.

Acquaintance Interview

YOUR BROTHER KNOWS SOMEONE AT A COMPANY about which you would like to learn more or where you believe you would like to work. He puts the two of you in touch. You might have met casually at a party or family event, but when you meet to discuss business, does the fact that you're already familiar with each other change how you are expected to behave? Are you expected to be more "chummy" than you might be otherwise, or should you maintain your interview persona? Where you meet might determine your performance. Below, a guide.

At the coffee shop: You don't have to wear a suit, Dingee says, "especially if your acquaintance knows you are unemployed. But put your best foot forward with your best business-casual dress."

"Come to my office": "If they offer [an invitation to their office], I would definitely take them up on it," Dingee says. It's your first step in the door. "It will also give you some insight into what the office environment is like and give you a feel for the culture." She advises that you make sure you are professionally dressed, as you can never be sure to whom you may be introduced in the corridor or at the elevator.

Find commonality: Try to find common ground with the person who is interviewing you. "Interviews are all about connections. With an acquaintance, allow for five to 10 minutes for small talk before getting down to the business of the interview," Brown-Volkman says. If you walk into someone's office and see a golf trophy, comment on it and certainly mention it if you are also a golfer. Research on the interviewer's interest and background can help, Dickerman says. "You have to make sure you know who your audience is."

Gossip girl: Never allow small talk to become too personal, especially when discussing colleagues in common. "You don't want to be negative," Dingee says. "There is always something positive that you can say about somebody. It's safe to be generic in your commentary. You don't know what the relationships behind the scenes are."

> Never allow small talk to become too personal, especially when dicussing colleagues in common.

Cocktails Interview

MEETING FOR COCKTAILS IS DIFFERENT from meeting for coffee or over lunch. The expectation is that you will meet in the evening and the situation will be less formal than the office—but not too informal.

Dressing for the occasion: Dress thoughtfully. For women, choices are greater but need to be made with care. "Obviously you shouldn't be dressed like you are going on a date. Tone it down a little bit. Be a little more conscious of necklines and colors." Brown-Volkman advises women to wear a dress with a jacket.

Selecting a drink: A beer? A glass of wine? A Rusty Nail? "Some get whatever their host gets," Dingee observes. "I tend to order what I am most comfortable with—a glass of wine. If there is a fairly casual crowd and most are going to order a beer, I might order a beer. Whatever you select is part of your personality—as long as you don't overindulge."

One-drink rule: "Whenever it is a business situation, I have a one-drink rule. Two drinks is the maximum," says Dingee, who as a former recruiter once received a job-search expense report in which a candidate ordered in excess of 10 drinks at one sitting. "That sends off some red flags. You want to be sociable, but you don't want to treat it like it's a frat party." Brown-Volkman says that she, too, would nurse one drink and suggests having a soda if you decide to move onto a second drink.

CHECKLIST: INTERVIEW PREP

LOGISTICS

○ **Face-to-face interviews:** Can you speak concisely about how to add value to the company?

- Have you researched the company's needs and challenges so you can ask at least three good questions?

- Do you know who will be interviewing you, and can you address specifically how your contributions will help them do their job?

○ **Telephone interviews:** Do you have a clear, quiet, dedicated line with a professional-sounding voicemail message where you can speak to hiring managers?

○ **Videoconferencing:** Should the need arise, are you equipped to conduct a videoconference interview in a clean, well-lighted space?

Be ready for interview questions like these:

ACHIEVEMENTS

○ What achievements are you most proud of in your career?

○ What is the most challenging thing you have ever done?

○ What are you good at? What are you not so good at?

○ Have you ever failed?

○ What has been your most/least rewarding role?

○ What led you to work in this field?

PERSONAL GROWTH

○ Why are you leaving your current job?

○ Describe your weaknesses. How do you compensate for them?

○ Describe your strengths. What is your greatest asset?

○ What would you like to be doing five years from now?

○ What will you do if you don't get this position?

○ What is most/least attractive about this position?

○ What motivates you?

PROBLEM-SOLVING

○ Tell me about a situation in which you had to adjust to changes over which you had no control. How did you handle it?

○ Tell me about a situation where you had to solve a difficult problem. What did you do? What was your thought process? What was the outcome? What do you wish you had done differently?

○ How do you handle stress?

○ Tell me about a time when you had to make a decision without all the information you needed. How did you handle it? Why? Were you happy with the outcome?

○ How will you prioritize multiple tasks?

○ Do you consider yourself a team player or do you think you work better solo? *(Hint: This could easily be a trick question.)*

MANAGEMENT STYLE

○ Describe your management style.

○ Does your management style fit with our corporate culture?

○ Give me an example of when you were able to successfully communicate with another person even when that individual may not have personally liked you (or vice versa). How did you handle it?

○ What is the toughest group that you have had to get cooperation from? What were the obstacles? How did you handle the situation? What were the reactions of the group members? What was the end result?

○ What makes you a leader rather than a follower?

○ How does your managerial style differ from others in your field?

CORPORATE GROWTH

○ How do you keep up with the industry? What kind of training and retraining have you undertaken in the past year?

○ What do you think are our company's primary competitive challenges?

○ Who do you see as our major competitors?

○ Do you have any questions for us? *(Hint: You should.)*

○ What do you know about our organization?

○ How do you see the future of our industry?

NITTY-GRITTY

○ In all honesty, what makes you so good?

○ Why should we hire you versus someone with the same skills and background?

○ How did you grow revenue?

○ Why are you interested in this job at this company?

○ What other types of jobs are you currently considering?

○ What do other managers think of your work?

○ Have you ever been asked to leave a position?

○ Tell me about the last time you fired someone.

○ Are you willing to travel?

○ What are your salary requirements?

○ How many hours a week do you typically work?

○ Do you hope to have any sort of flexible work arrangement, including telecommuting and/or flex time?

○ Do you have any concerns about this position?

INTERVIEWS

Interview Date	Company/Agency	Job Interviewing for (if applicable)	Link to Job

Interviewer Name/Title	Phone	Date Sent Thank-You	Comments

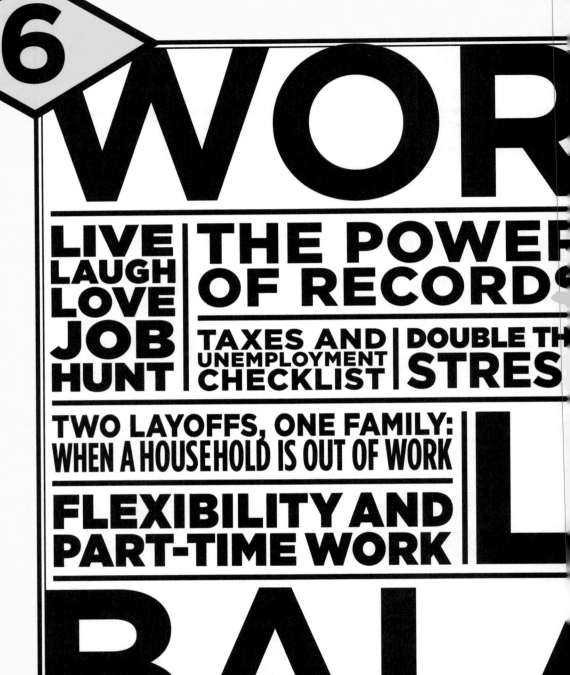

WOR

LIVE LAUGH LOVE JOB HUNT

THE POWER OF RECORDS

TAXES AND UNEMPLOYMENT CHECKLIST

DOUBLE TH STRES

TWO LAYOFFS, ONE FAMILY: WHEN A HOUSEHOLD IS OUT OF WORK

FLEXIBILITY AND PART-TIME WORK

L

BALA

K

HOW MANY HOURS A WEEK SHOULD YOU JOB SEEK?

YOUR LAYOFF

YOUR BRAIN: HOW TO GET OUT OF YOUR OWN WAY

OW TO THINK CREATIVELY

YOU OWE | **AVOID JOINING THE MASS DEPRESSION**

OW ANXIETY TRIGGERS A SENSE OF ALERTNESS

FE | **STAYING HEALTHY THROUGH TROUBLED TIMES**

NCE

My name is Matthew Rothenberg and I'm a layoff survivor. I knew the day was coming for months. I understood the economic and operational realities at my company; I'd even directed some early phases of the downsizing. I'd started my job search well in advance. I'd built a solid landing pad that included plenty of contract work and some pre-planning with my family.

I'd even started moving personal effects discreetly out of my office ... shades of "The Great Escape"! But there's no way to prepare completely for the moment when you're told to box up your stuff, turn in your equipment and leave the premises. The anxiety and self-doubt it provokes need to be respected—and channeled in positive ways.

In my case, my regimen included visits to the family doctor, who did indeed diagnose and medicate mild hypertension. It meant monitoring my daily routine to stay busy and engaged with the rest of the working world. And it meant keeping very close tabs on warning signs of depression.

The result? My time "between engagements" was one of the most rewarding of my adult life. I kept money coming in, and I had a real opportunity to re-engage with my family (the real reason for that paycheck).

Your Layoff, Your Brain: Don't Let Stress Paralyze You

GRACE BARRY DID EVERYTHING RIGHT. After being laid off from a high-level IT position at a government agency, she got right to work at the job of finding a job.

"I didn't anticipate having a difficult time," says Barry. "I knew that looking for a job was a full-time job, but I'm very organized about it. I take advice. I went and re-wrote my resume so that it was more achievement-based; I read the books; I signed up for TheLadders; I scoured the Internet; and, at one time, I had more than 100 applications out there."

Barry adds that, through it all, she never stopped networking.

The result of doing "everything right" for about seven months? One interview.

Barry did receive an offer as a result of that inteview—but the job was in financial services and the offer fell through when the industry collapsed.

Looking for a job after being involuntarily let go from a position is difficult under any circumstances. In today's economy a job search can be prolonged, and the effects can be even more pronounced on your body, mind and spirit.

"It's a big challenge to your capacity to adapt, just like a prolonged illness is a challenge or going through war is a challenge," says Michael Jolkovski PhD, a psychologist and psychoanalyst in Falls Church, Va., and principal at Working Through, a consultancy focused on helping creative teams work effectively together.

When a person loses a job, he is likely to experience anger, stress, and feelings of anxiety and depression. Left unchecked, these feelings can become detrimental to a person's physical and mental health, hindering the ability to search effectively for a new job. In short, our natural responses may work against us.

How Anxiety Triggers a Sense of Alertness

IN ITSELF, ANXIETY ISN'T A BAD THING. Indeed, it's a prime motivator when it comes to tackling challenges. In fact, medical explanations are illuminating on the subject.

"People do have physiological changes when they get anxious—their fight-or-flight system gets going and, biologically, through evolution, if we perceive a threat we need to fight it or run away or, in some cases, freeze and hope that it ignores us," according to Kathryn J. Fraser, a psychiatrist and associate professor of psychiatry at the University of New Mexico School of Medicine in Albuquerque.

"Unfortunately, the way our culture is, we don't have people to fight or to run away from. We've got bigger, more nebulous things." According to Fraser, physical responses to an involuntary job loss can include sleeplessness, tension leading to headaches and stomachaches, and panic attacks that generate myriad physical symptoms. She argues that anxiety symptoms, such as heightened senses, might be useful to propel us in the short term, but they can lead to depression if experienced over longer periods.

"If people get more into depression it's partly because of what's called the hypo-thalamic-pituitary-adrenal axis, abbreviated as HPA," she explains. "It has to do with cortisol—that's a part of our endocrine system that gets going. This is very useful in short-term threatening situations, but with longer-term anxiety, like with losing a job, that kind of response predisposes people to depression."

This can lead to a destructive Catch-22.

"If [people are] anxious and depressed and can't sleep," says Fraser, "they might be less able to do the things they need to do to find another job or to at least keep their spirits high enough to feel good about other things that may be going on in their lives."

Experts agree that external support should be sought if these symptoms worsen or extend over time, or if feelings of hopelessness set in. "We all feel stress—but the shift ... to anxiety or depression typically comes when you start to experience feelings of hopelessness, and some of the things you used to enjoy you no longer enjoy," says Kevin Skinner, a marriage and family therapist. "And so you shift gears from, 'I'm going to make it through this—I don't know the answer, but I'm going to make it through this,' to, 'I don't know if we're going to make it.' "

"You need to have some anxiety—we all have some anxiety," says Justin Tobin, a psychotherapist in Chicago. "If we don't have any anxiety then we'll never be able to meet any of our own goals. ... It's when we start to buy into the belief that there's only six months left—what if I don't find something? Those thoughts can push on the anxiety and make the anxiety uncontrollable."

Avoid Joining the Mass Depression

COPING WITH THE FEELINGS that go along with a job loss is challenging under any circumstances, but job seekers find themselves dealing with negative group-think and perhaps even a mass depression.

Fraser takes the notion a step further, saying that too much exposure to television and the Internet—regardless of the program—can have mental as well as physical consequences.

"I think it's important that people limit their time [watching] the TV," he says. "There are actual studies that show that too much TV goes along with increased depression. And part of it is, physically, people are just sitting there, watching something, and our bodies were not meant to do that. Again, back to evolutionary psychology, we need to be out running around and doing physical exercise."

In fact, experts tell TheLadders time and again that regular exercise and eating right are key to maintaining the healthy mind and body that will be required for an arduous job search. "We all sweat from anxiety," says Elizabeth Friedman, a clinical psychologist in New York. "It is way better to sweat from a good workout. There is all kinds of evidence that exercise releases all kinds of good stuff in your brain and makes you more positive."

Indeed, people will have to work hard to overcome the repeated rejection that can come with an extended job search. "The mind has to change to the concept of, 'It's going to take me a while to find a job,'" says Skinner, who also shares his expert advice at MyExpertSolution.com.

"[Think], 'It's not a matter of if, but a matter of when I get that new job. And until then, I'm going to be hitting up against a lot of rejection.' And we don't deal with rejection very well as human beings, especially when it has to do with our finances and being able to provide for our families."

Jolkovski agrees. "It's sort of like the entrepreneur's mentality, where people are doing something and the success is uncertain," he says. "Just like certain salespeople—if they get a 1 percent response rate, then they're doing well. They have to have the mentality to make 99 calls and say, 'Well, there's one more down,' instead of saying, 'Oh, I've been rejected 99 times.'"

How to Think Creatively

EXPERTS ALSO SUGGEST THAT JOB SEEKERS make use of some creative thinking. In today's market, your next job might not be the same as the one from which you were let go—in function, responsibility or pay. But that may have to be OK and, in some cases, can be a positive life change.

"Try and flip it around as an opportunity," Friedman suggests. "There are jobs out there—not as many [as there were], but there are jobs. You could find something a little different, and that's cool. Change is growth. For many of us, change can be a very scary thing. For people who are successful, change is usually a very positive challenge and, potentially, an exciting thing. To do a job that's a tiny bit different or even a lot different—but within your skill set in any case—that's kind of nice."

After her lone job offer fell through and nothing else "hit" despite her best efforts, Grace Barry decided it was time for something a lot different. She set out to build a consultancy of her own and began doing research and networking for the new business. During that process—and completely out of left field—a person she had gone to for advice recruited and hired her to his company.

"[The position is] actually in business development, and I had only been on the engineering side, and it's certainly at quite a salary cut," says Barry of her new job. "But I'm working today, and I'm very, very happy to be working. ... You always hear, 'Keep networking, keep networking'—I never stopped networking. I never stopped doing what I was supposed to do. I did everything that I read about, everything I heard about. It was almost like an act of desperation got me someplace where I could interview for a job." Setting expectations is key to maintaining a sense of hope. It may take a while, and your journey won't be exactly like Barry's, or any one person's. It will be your own, and reminding yourself that you are the one in control of the situation can be the key to keeping your composure.

When Job Loss Shakes Your Identity—and Confidence

ONE BIG CHALLENGE SEASONED PROFESSIONALS FACE when they've lost their jobs is that they've also lost a big piece of their identity. "Being out of work is a terrible feeling," says clinical psychologist Friedman. "We identify at least part of our self with what we do. Hopefully it's not all of our self-definition, but it is a big part of it. So we lose our grounding, our footing, in certain ways. 'Who am I? Where am I going? What do I do tomorrow morning at 8:00? Do I get up? Do I stay in bed?' "

Staying in bed is not the right answer! In fact, sticking to a routine and applying control when and where you can is key. "Take one day to feel terrible, and then get moving," Friedman says. "It's very important to keep basic routines. You can't suddenly be up all night long watching 'Law & Order.' Get up in the morning; take a shower. If you're a guy, shave; if you're a woman, do your hair. Send out a million e-mails, contact all of your friends."

A sense of identity loss can affect a person's relationships and family dynamics as well. "When you've lost a job, you start to question your own identity," says Skinner. "Sometimes if it's an extended job loss, you begin to feel guilty, especially if it's affecting your family, and maybe your wife has to go back to work. You start to feel like, 'What's wrong with me?' And it's not about that."

What it is about, says Skinner, is reaching out to others and focusing on realistic solutions. "The best thing we can do in these times is get additional support. You might have to turn to family for support. You might have to go live somewhere else—downgrade your home, downgrade your cars. The resilient people are going to say, 'I'm going to find a solution—I'm a person who finds solutions to problems.' "

How to Conserve Credit for a Job Search

DURING A LAYOFF, ACCESS TO CREDIT can be your lifeline to keeping the lights on, but it's also crucial to getting your next job. There is no way around it: Looking for a job costs money. BillShrink.com, a bill-management software maker based in Redwood City, Calif., researched the cost of the typical six-month job search for residents in Los Angeles County.

While the prices are not transferable nationwide, the items are:

- **Gas:** $500 (based on an average commute of 33 miles to an interview once a week for six months)
- **Clothing:** $775 (one suit, one shirt/blouse, one tie, one pair of shoes)
- **Haircut:** $50
- **Phone:** $780 ($130 monthly phone bill for six months)
- **TheLadders.com:** $120 (a six-month subscription)
  TOTAL: $2,225

Keeping some room on your credit may give you the breathing room you need to keep looking for a job. Macro-economic factors and your own income may collude to lower your available credit.

Live, Laugh, Love, Job Hunt

FOR MOST OF US, THE WORK/LIFE BALANCE is a delicate one. We carefully mete out our time, resources and energy to our bosses, co-workers, spouses, kids, parents, friends, pets, charities and—if all goes perfectly as planned—ourselves. The slightest change can upset the balance. A big change— such as a job loss—has the potential to bring everything crashing down.

In today's economy, a job loss can be especially upsetting to the work/life balance because the resulting job hunt may extend for several months. With jobs scarce and job hunters plentiful, looking for work becomes a full-time job. However, unlike

---

WHEN TO SEEK OUTSIDE SUPPORT

The loss of a job hits both your pocketbook and your very identity. Negative feelings are only natural after being laid off and going through a job search—especially in the current economic climate—but there are some red flags that indicate professional help should be sought, especially when you experience symptoms over prolonged periods of time.

- Depressed mood
- Insomnia
- Significant weight gain or weight loss
- Withdrawal from activities
- Withdrawal from family
- Increased substance use
- Being set off by things that didn't affect you before
- Feelings of shame
- Feelings of helplessness
- Feelings of hopelessness

most full-time positions, the job hunt offers no pay, no security and—perhaps most significantly—no structured time off. This makes it more difficult to maintain that delicate balance we call life.

When you're on the job search, you don't get vacation time or even a lunch hour. It becomes a personal and financial necessity to balance your other responsibilities and keep those unexpected events like family emergencies from upsetting your job search.

Betty P. knows this only too well. She lost her position as an EDI consultant at a pharmaceutical wholesaler because a required relocation would have meant moving her elderly mother—who was in the care of her and her family—from Wisconsin to Ohio.

With 18 months' notice to prepare for the change, Betty used the time to get her resume and affairs in order. But she couldn't predict that her mother would suddenly take ill, require more intensive care and pass away just a month after she left the company.

Betty also has three busy children (one in college); a husband who works in the real-estate business (an industry struggling to get its footing); and health issues of her own. With all of this going on, searching for a job has been "fatiguing."

Betty has sent out dozens of resumes and is working with a job-placement consultant. She says she has become frustrated with the inhuman quality of the process, where applicants must be an exact match and where thoughtful, heartfelt applications receive an automated response—if they receive any response at all.

The Power of Records

SO HOW DOES SHE KEEP IT ALL TOGETHER?

Organization is key. For example, after hearing from a friend who had to fake her way through a telephone response to an application because the friend wasn't sure which job was being referred to, Betty has started keeping careful records.

"I keep a spreadsheet," she says. "It includes the date I applied for a job, the job title and where I heard about it." She also copies descriptions of the jobs she applies for in a Microsoft Word document so she'll "be ready if someone calls." Recruiters also recommend job seekers keep track of which version of their resume and cover letter went with which application to be sure they're not surprised in an interview by details omitted from one version of their resume but present on another.

Betty is also setting job-hunting goals. For example, she attempts to send out two or more applications every week, and she is now going back and following up on applications she has already submitted.

AROUND THE WEB: READ MORE ABOUT IT

ADAA.org

Dedicated to the prevention, treatment and cure of anxiety disorders, the Anxiety Disorders Association of America Web site provides descriptions of different anxiety disorders, self-tests, recommendations for treatment, resources and case studies.

BrainSource.com

Your brain on stress is described at BrainSource.com, which also provides tools and resources for coping with stress.

HelpGuide.org

This is a site designed to help people "understand, prevent and resolve life's challenges." The site provides information on the symptoms and types of depression, as well as recommendations for where to find help.

MayoClinic.com

An adjustment disorder is a severe emotional reaction to a life change. The Mayo Clinic's Web site offers valuable information on the symptoms, causes, risk factors, complications and treatment for adjustment disorders, as well as advice on prevention and when to seek medical advice.

MedlinePlus.com

A service of the National Library of Medicine and the National Institutes of Health, MedlinePlus provides information to help answer health-related questions. The site provides useful recommendations for managing stress as well as an interactive tutorial that illustrates how stress affects the body's systems.

How Many Hours a Week Should You Job Seek?

"AS A JOB SEEKER, YOU NEED YOUR OWN PLAN or a time budget each week," says Raoul Encinas, a board member of the Scottsdale Job Network and vice president of Preod, a professional services firm based in Princeton, N.J. "If you have other demands on your time, then budgeting five, 15, 25 hours a week for your job-seeking activity is fine. You then need to tailor your weekly goals to your budget. If your normal weekly goal is to have 10 one-on-one networking meetings a week, but you can only allocate 20 hours, then change your goal to five meetings a week. That way, at the end of the week you don't beat yourself up for not making progress on your job-search goals."

And all those other people vying for your time and attention? Enlist them in the process, says Katy Piotrowski of Career Solutions Group. "If your job search is truly a priority, reflect that in your behavior," Piotrowski advises. "Delegate chores to other family members so that you have the time to invest in your next career step.

Remember, your advancement will benefit them also."

Experts also advise job seekers to be open and honest with family and friends about what they are going through and to set realistic expectations. "Job seekers should talk to their children about the realities of today's economy and about how a job search can sometimes take a long time. It may be difficult for them to realize that you may not be able to get a job tomorrow and that it may take prolonged effort over an extended period of time to get the right job for you," says Sharon Reed Abboud, who wrote *"All Moms Work: Short-Term Career Strategies for Long-Range Success."*

Stay Healthy, Stay Sharp

ONE PERSON WHO OFTEN IS NEGLECTED during the job search is the job seeker.

Mental-health and career experts advocate making time for exercise and favorite activities, no matter how desperate the search becomes. In fact, the more stressful the search, the more important these activities may be, as they can prevent job seekers from entering a state of depression.

But remaining active is also an important part of maintaining that elusive work/life balance during the job search.

"What I do when I get tired is get up and do something physical—weed, move flowers, mow the lawn," Betty says. "It takes me away from the stress of the job search." Betty has also been taking the time to create family pictorials, tracing the history of family members, including her mother. She says this has been a healthy distraction. "Family albums bring you back to what's important in life."

Two Layoffs, One Family: When a Household Is Out of Work

WHAT HAPPENS WHEN TWO INCOMES BECOME NO INCOMES? Just ask the Gosses of McLean, Va. Charley Gosse was laid off from his job as chief financial officer at a nearby private school and has been in search of a job ever since. Laura Gosse was laid off about a year later from her job as vice president of an online marketing company.

Laura and Charley were once dual wage-earners in a two-income family that also includes two young daughters. Now they are tightening their belts to make ends meet on dwindling severances, savings and unemployment benefits while conducting dual job searches for a no-income family.

They're not alone. Hundreds of thousands of two-income families became no-income families in the past decade, according to the Bureau of Labor Statistics. For the Gosses and others facing two layoffs and two job searches, the experience requires more than just a plan to save money. A dual job search, say experts and families who have experienced it, requires a different job-search strategy. Any plan must support and coordinate resume writing, interview scheduling and traveling. It must also take into account potential decisions about whether to relocate or accept an offer that could change life for every member of the family.

Adding Structure and Support Helps Ease Stress Levels

WHEN CHARLEY WAS LAID OFF, the family immediately went into cost-cutting mode. Laura's salary covered expenses, but she and Charley didn't know how long he would be out of work and so they went into "complete savings mode."

The couple cut back on lots of different things. They eliminated dinners out and vacations, and they let their live-in au pair go, since Charley was home and could care for the children while Laura worked.

When Laura was laid off, they took belt-tightening to a new level. "We both received severance of different, varying lengths, and [by that point] we'd been frugal for a year," she says. "So, it was just like, 'OK, let's tighten the belt a little more.' "

The bigger challenge was managing what was now two ongoing job searches.

"We both started looking for full-time work," Laura says. "Charley was staying home because of my situation, and when that changed, we both had to concentrate on looking for jobs." Laura says the parallel job hunt got off to a bit of a rocky start. "We were both doing our job hunting. Our younger daughter would come home from preschool and we didn't really have any structure. We felt bad that we were both trying to figure out our way and she was just kind of playing by herself."

Realizing that more structure was key to managing two job searches and a family, Laura and her husband worked out a schedule where each worked at the job hunt every other day while the other held down the home front.

"That's the model," says Donna Spellman, director of Self-Sufficiency Services at Family Centers of Greenwich, Conn., a human-services agency that, among many other things, provides career and family counseling. "If one person is staying behind with the kids, focusing on keeping things moving along smoothly, that person is creating space for the other person to do their thing," Spellman says. "And perhaps tomorrow or the next day, they switch. But it means that everybody's truly doing his or her part. They're not scrambling, and they're not saying, 'I thought you were going to stay home!' It's not about that."

Flexibility and Part-Time Work

WHILE LAURA AND CHARLEY FOUND THAT STRUCTURE WAS KEY, they also learned that they had to remain flexible. Their ability to adapt was put to the test when Laura obtained a part-time job that took her away from home three days a week. Now, "The days that I am home, I give [Charley] those days to do what he needs to do so we can keep moving forward," she says.

Laura added that she and Charley "switch off" when necessary—for example, when an interview or meeting comes up. Spellman says it is critical that both job-hunting partners demonstrate this kind of adaptability. "It will happen that somebody's going to get a call that's going to be very spur of the moment—'I've got an interview and I've gotta go.' The partners have to be flexible as much as possible."

Laura and Charley have been working together so that each of their job-hunting strategies, resources and skills can be leveraged by the other. For example, Laura showed Charley how to use the LinkedIn network, and the couple reviews each other's resume and cover letter before sending them out.

Another no-income family, Lee and Cheryl H., also found themselves sharing the load. Lee and Cheryl both lost their Kentucky state jobs when the governor they worked for was not re-elected. Lee says Cheryl and he were not terribly worried at the time they were let go, as Cheryl found a good job with benefits shortly thereafter.

However, that job happened to be in the automotive industry, and Cheryl was laid off during industry cutbacks. Lee, who says he and Cheryl have extended their job search and will consider relocating, stressed the importance of mutual support in a two-person job search.

"We're extremely fortunate in that we have a wonderful, solid, strong relationship," he says. "As a matter of fact, when she was laid off, I think it actually helped me because it helped me stop focusing just on myself. I had to be strong for her at that point."

That kind of mutual support has bolstered the dual job-hunting Gosses, as well. "There's a lot of stress when one parent is out of a job; when two parents are out of a job, clearly that puts a lot of different stresses on the whole thing," Laura says. "But [my husband and I] are compatible, and we work well with each other. "

Lee says he and Cheryl, who have three grown children, enjoy their time together but also recognize the need for time apart. "Being together 24/7 has not been an issue for us," Lee said. "But we do realize that there are times when we need a few hours apart. No matter how much you love each other, you need a little break once in a while."

Maintaining a positive attitude can be the difference between landing a job and not landing it.

Keeping Perspective

IN TODAY'S ECONOMY, THE JOB SEARCH CAN BE PROLONGED, a fact that is all too familiar to both families. Experts stress the importance of remembering that the situation is temporary.

"The mind has to change the concept of, 'It's going to take me a while to find a job,'" says Skinner. "It's not a matter of 'if,' but a matter of 'when' I get that new job."

Family Centers' Spellman says she understands that it can be difficult to maintain a positive attitude under such difficult circumstances, but that such positivity could be the difference between landing a job and not landing it.

"Attitude is three-quarters of it," Spellman says. "It's not just, 'Do you have the hard skills?'; it's 'Do you click on a personality level?' And so a healthy attitude and a positive, upbeat personality are going to really carry an enormous amount of weight—both at home and in the workplace."

Yet when both members of a couple are out of work, there may be no financial fallback. Even couples with healthy savings and severance can't help but wonder and worry about making ends meet. When those ends aren't quite coming together, it's important to put aside feelings of guilt and blame. Remember that you didn't ask for this situation and that it won't last forever.

If your job hunt is getting you down, take the weekend and blow off some steam. Go duck hunting. Read a trashy novel. Then come back next week with newfound power and stamina.

CHECKLIST: TAXES AND UNEMPLOYMENT

YOU'VE BEEN LAID OFF and you're watching your pennies. You need to focus on your job search now—but to keep on the right side of the IRS, here's a simple panel of financial levers you'll need to pull along the way. A couple of notes before we start: Tax laws can change year to year, so make sure to review specific questions with a pro. Also, the advice here applies specifically to federal taxes; things like mileage may vary state to state and town to town. Unless otherwise noted, the material here was drawn from IRS Publication 17. And in case you're wondering, the cost of this book is tax deductible.

1. SEVERANCE, VACATION AND SICK PAY

Why it matters:

Severance and any payments for accrued vacation and sick time are considered part of regular wages for the year in question. That means taxes, Social Security and Medicare should be withheld at the same rates they were while you were employed.

What to watch for:

○ Vacation and sick time are generally paid out in one lump sum with taxes withheld. Make sure that's true for you.

○ Some employers will offer a laid-off employee the option to receive their severance at once or in installments. Will scheduled payments stretch into another calendar year? That could change your income for the year and thus your tax liability.

○ Have you maxed out your FICA contributions? If so, it might be best to take a lump sum instead.

2. OUTPLACEMENT SERVICES

Why it matters:

If you're lucky enough to receive outplacement services as part of your separation from your employer (such as training in interview techniques or help writing a resume), the IRS may consider that taxable income.
(IRS Publication 15-A)

What to watch for:

Outplacement services should be **tax-exempt** if:

○ The services are based on need.

○ Your former employer can claim a business benefit, such as improved employee morale or public relations. (Talk to your HR department to get the skinny.)

○ You would be able to deduct the costs anyway. (Ask your accountant.)

2. OUTPLACEMENT SERVICES (CONTINUED)

Outplacement services are **taxable** if:

○ Your employer offers outplacement services in lieu of a reduced severance. In that case, you must report the difference as income.

○ The IRS instructs employers to withhold taxes as part of severance, but double-check with your former company to make sure they've connected those dots. (By the way, you can probably deduct the difference.)

3. SUPPLEMENTAL UNEMPLOYMENT BENEFITS

Why it matters:

If your former employer agrees to extend you benefits such as low-interest loans, or use of a vehicle or housing, the IRS will consider those items taxable income. *(IRS Publication 15-A)*

What to watch for:

○ Your former employer is unlikely to withhold taxes for these benefits. Check with your employer and book time with a tax attorney to determine what items are tax-exempt and be prepared to cover the taxes on those that aren't.

4. 401(K), IRA AND QUALIFIED RETIREMENT PLANS

Why it matters:

If you've lost your job, you're likely to lose your enrollment in the company's 401(k) program. How you handle the funds that come your way can affect your tax exposure.

What to watch for:

○ Distributions from IRAs and 401(k)s are tax-exempt, but the clock is ticking: You have 60 days to move all or part of it to another eligible retirement account without penalty. After that, the money may be taxed up to 20 percent.

○ Younger than 60? Any taxable portion not rolled over may be subject to an additional 10 percent penalty on early distributions, and even steeper penalties may apply. Move it or lose it.

○ Some 401(k)s allow you to withdraw a temporary loan or a hardship distribution to cover the bills. Be aware: An interest-bearing loan is tax exempt, but a withdrawal is subject to taxes and penalties.

5. UNEMPLOYMENT COMPENSATION

Why it matters:

Unemployment compensation is taxable income.

What to watch for:

O You have a choice here: You may decide to with-hold 10 percent (the minimum U.S. tax) of your unemployment benefits for federal taxes *(Form W-4V)*; you can pay estimated quarterly tax; or you can pay it all come April 15. Be aware: Whichever option you choose, you will be taxed based on your gross income for the year. Chances are you will owe more for the year than the 10 percent you paid.

Here's an example: Say you earned $5,000 in unemployment during the year and paid $500 at the 10 percent rate, but your total income for the year was $75,000 (in taxable wages). In that case, you are still in the 25 percent tax bracket and would be obligated to pay an additional $750 in taxes on your unemployment.

O Some companies, unions and individuals arrange for private unemployment insurance, called "supplemental unemployment."

O Payments are considered wages and are taxed at a standard rate. The original amount you paid into the fund is tax exempt.

6. MORTGAGE AND PAYMENT ASSISTANCE

Why it matters:

While between jobs, you may use payment-protection plans and programs that help cover your bills. Some of these are tax exempt.

What to watch for:

O Mortgage-assistance payments covered by the National Housing Act are tax exempt.

O Property-tax relief and payments made by a state or municipality to help pay utility bills are generally tax exempt.

O Payment-protection (creditor) insurance, including programs offered by automakers, may be tax exempt, but slow down and check with your provider and accountant—it may be considered income.

7. SELLING INVESTMENTS AND ASSETS TO PAY THE BILLS

Why it matters:

If you sell investments and property to help pay the bills, the proceeds will most likely be considered taxable income.

What to watch for:

○ For investment properties, taxable income depends on the type of property, its value and how long you've owned it. It may be ordinary income subject to regular income tax rates, or it may be considered a capital gain, subject to a separate rate. *(IRS Publication 544)*

○ If you sell your primary residence, profits may be tax exempt up to $250,000 ($500,000 for married and filing jointly). *(IRS Publication 523)*

8. SELF-EMPLOYMENT

Why it matters:

If you choose to work for hire during your layoff, there are a whole new set of rules that govern self-employment.

What to watch for:

○ If you work as a contractor or open your own business, you will need to file a 1099 form and pay out for taxes, Social Security and Medicare.

○ If you plan to work for yourself for an extended period of time and expect to pay more than $1,000 in taxes on earned income, the IRS recommends you make quarterly estimated tax payments. Like payroll withholding tax, you may still owe money at the end of the year, or you may receive a refund.

9. DEDUCTIONS

Why it matters:

The rules change when your income changes. You can take advantage of deductions previously unavailable—but handle them with care.

What to watch for:

○ **Earned Income Tax Credit**
You may not have qualified in prior years, but your reduced income may meet the standard. Talk to an accountant or check the IRS EITC assistant to find out.

○ **Health Care**
If you're paying for your own medical bills or health insurance, your expenditures can probably be itemized deductions. An accountant can tell you if income qualifications apply.

Premium payments for COBRA (continued health insurance) are generally not tax

9. DEDUCTIONS (CONTINUED)

deductible, but under the American Recovery and Re-investment Act, you may be able to put most of the burden on your employer, if you qualify.

○ **Job-Hunting Expenses and Deductions**
If you're looking for a job in your current field, you may deduct certain expenses related to the search, including:

   ○ Membership fees to job boards such as TheLadders

   ○ Career services such as resume assistance and interview preparation

   ○ Travel to interviews

   ○ Phone calls related to the search

   ○ The cost of copying and preparing your resume

   ○ Child care (or care for other dependents) *(IRS Publication 529)*

○ **Moving Expenses**
If you move more than 50 miles for a new job, you may be able to deduct your moving expenses, but there are rules about the distance and timing of the move, and the job must be related to your current field. *(IRS Publication 521)*

○ **Education and Training**
Tuition and fees for most classes and training programs are likely to be tax deductible. *(IRS Publication 970)*

○ **Home Office**
If you decide to perform contract work or start your own business during a layoff, you may be able to deduct some of the costs of maintaining a home office. You must dedicate a portion of your home exclusively to business use.

IF YOU OWE

If you can't pay, the IRS recommends you nevertheless file a return on time and send what you can. You will still be charged interest on the amount owed and assessed late-payment penalties, but you'll avoid the penalty for failing to file a tax return. You can also arrange at that time for a payment plan.

CHECKLIST: STAYING HEALTHY THROUGH TROUBLED TIMES

Being let go from a job is difficult under any circumstances. Mental-health experts and people who have been through it agree that the following advice will help you maintain your emotional and physical health during what can be a stressful time.

○ Exercise regularly.

○ Eat a healthy diet.

○ Maintain a regular schedule, especially when it comes to sleep.

○ Stay away from anything that can dull your edge, such as alcohol.

○ Don't try and go it alone. Connect regularly with other people, both in your professional and personal circles. If all of your connections were through your job, consider seeking out religious or community organizations.

○ Make yourself useful. Reaching out to others during this time is one way to help you feel valuable—and valued.

○ Limit your exposure to television and the Internet. Sitting passively while consuming bad news is detrimental in many ways.

○ Seek out free services in your community. Many people who have been working don't realize that there is a safety net out there—everything from the library to mental-health services.

○ There are many things you can't control right now, so focus on the things you can: how many resumes you send out, how many phone calls you make and so on.

○ Don't put all your eggs in one basket. If you pin all of your hopes on one "perfect" job, you have to start all over again if you don't get it.

○ Think outside the box. Your next job may not be the same—in function or in pay—as the one from which you were laid off.

○ Count your blessings. There are worse things than losing a job.

IS A GOOD JOB

TITLE WORTH GIVING UP SOME SALARY?

INTERVIEW AND NEGOTIATE LIKE A LAWYER

JUSTIFY AND RATIONALIZE

DO YOU HAVE TO REVEAL YOUR INCOME?

SA

NEGO

TIA

HOW TO TURN A JOB OFFER INTO A RAISE

MAKE SMALL CONCESSIONS

STEPS TO LEVERAGE
COUNTEROFFER FOR A
ARGER SALARY

MAKE
THE
FIRST
OFFER

ARY

DODGE AND DEFLECT

O-BE REAL

TION

A compensation package is a brew of facts and figures that you've got to season to your personal taste—after all, you hope to be living off this recipe for a while!

There's base salary, of course, but any senior executive will also consider bonuses, vacation time, benefits, equity and other measures of value. Meanwhile, there are less tangible considerations to weigh, including the length of your commute, the hours you're expected to put in, flexibility in your schedule and any costs you will incur to take up the job.

And while it may seem remote right now, don't forget to consider an exit strategy. How closely is your personal compensation tied to the performance of the company, and what can your prospective employer do to guarantee you won't be left in the lurch if things don't go as well as both of you hope?

Once you've figured out what you want in terms of compensation, you'll need to decide how much to reveal to that prospective employer. If you've reached the negotiation stage, the company clearly recognizes that you can bring value to the role for which you've auditioned. Now ask, do your requirements match their interest? How high has the employer assessed the worth of your personal brand, and when is it the optimal time to find out?

Do You Have to Reveal Your Income?

FEW PROFESSIONAL CONVERSATIONS ARE MORE AWKWARD than those about how much money you make. For job seekers, though, salary and compensation history isn't just an uncomfortable topic to avoid with a relative. It's often a make-or-break moment in a long-sought job interview.

You probably don't want to answer the question about your salary history at all. Most employment lawyers and job-interview experts say your best bet is to dodge the question and focus on your potential value to the company, not your current paycheck.

There is no legal protection to prohibit a recruiter or hiring manager from asking the question or pressing you to provide an answer. So prepare an answer that you can support but that also maintains your control of the situation.

There is a significant risk of either pricing yourself out of a job or low-balling a potential offer, according to David A. Earle, managing partner at Staffing.org, an analyst company that measures recruiting trends.

"If you really need the job, you're at a disadvantage; if you end up taking an offer that's too low, you're going to find out about it around the water cooler," Earle says. "If you're an in-demand candidate, it's a different psychological situation. Then there's nothing wrong with walking in and saying 'I make $170,000 where I am and would need at least $190,000 to even think about leaving.'"

Hiring managers are under enormous pressure to keep salaries down. But if they press too hard, it might be a sign the candidate should remove the opportunity from serious consideration. "If I got that [salary] question in an interview, I'd think, 'This guy's trying to get me for the lowest price he can get,' and I'd have to wonder if I wanted to work for him," says Ed McGlynn, managing director of Financial Recruiters LLC and a former senior vice president at Lehman Brothers.

Whether the question is asked at all and what part it plays in the negotiation depend largely on leverage—something few professionals have in the job market right now, according to Stephen E. Seckler, president of Seckler Legal Consulting in Newton, Mass., a consultancy that advises law firms on how to manage their businesses more effectively.

"It's very difficult to not answer that question if it's asked straight out," Seckler says. "It's not usually to your advantage to answer, but saying you don't feel like answering sends the signal that you're not a cooperative person. They're screening you partly to see if [you're] someone they want to work with, and that could create a problematic impression."

Most negotiation experts say the first person to speak a number or make an offer is at a disadvantage because they give the other party a target to shoot down—in this case telling a job candidate the number is far too high for the position or budget, whether it is or not.

Victoria Pynchon, a veteran litigator-turned-mediator at ADR Services, emphasizes the importance of preparation. Do your homework, and be able to back up your negotiating position with evidence from Salary.com, professional association surveys and other sources that provide hard, competitive numbers.

Dodge and Deflect

REFUSING TO ANSWER WHEN ASKED POINT-BLANK or lying about how much you were paid in order to push up the amount of any possible offer is the absolute worst option for a job seeker, McGlynn, Earle and Seckler agreed.

"Part of the company's due diligence on you is going to be checking references, and there's a good chance they're going to find out either then or later what your real salary was," Seckler explains. "You're basically starting out by giving the company a reason to fire you if they ever want to, even if there wasn't cause for it then."

The best way to deal with the question is to deflect it. If you can't, break your whole compensation package down to show where the value lies. Your salary might have been X, but your bonus was Y for specific accomplishments you can name.

Being honest doesn't mean being vulnerable. "It's very important to know where you stand, and there's far too much information available online about salaries and compensation to not know how you compared," Earle points out. "If you made $142,000 and you know damn well that this position rarely pays less than $130,000—and you're willing to take that—then if they come back with an offer of $120,000, you know that's outside your playing field and they're just trying to screw you."

Interview and Negotiate Like a Lawyer

LAWYERS ARE TRAINED NOT ONLY TO ARGUE a position but persuade judges, juries and even adversaries to try to see things their ways. What can they teach job seekers about convincing a hiring manager to give them the job (and the money) they're after?

According to Pynchon, the first thing to remember when taking advice from a lawyer on how to persuade and negotiate is that your end goal is very different from a lawyer's end game. When lawyers argue, their goals are to win, not generally to meet the other party halfway or form a lasting bond.

"You negotiate based on positions—I'm right, and you're wrong, and here are

10,000 reasons why you're wrong and I should get the biggest share of the pie," she says. That's not a bad approach in the courtroom or across the negotiating table from an opponent after the lines have been drawn and the first shots fired in a dispute.

"It's not so good in a job interview when what you're trying to do is establish a relationship," says Seckler, who spent 15 years as a legal recruiter. A salary negotiation isn't a conflict to be resolved, Pynchon says. There is a lot of push and pull, but what you're building is a relationship that you both hope will last a long time, not a scorched-earth business deal. Still, there is more back-and-forth in a good negotiation than most Americans are comfortable with.

What follows are some of our favorite "legal" tips on negotiating.

Don't negotiate with yourself. "One of the things they did teach us at law school about negotiating is, don't bargain against yourself," Pynchon says. "If you say you want $190,000 and the other person says that's well beyond the range, don't come back and say, 'How about $150,000?' Wait for their response; don't bargain yourself down."

Justify and rationalize. Always give a reason, preferably a good one, for what you're asking for. If you don't have a good reason, give a bad one. In studies of human behavior, people offering a ridiculous reason for asking a favor have nearly the same success rate as those offering logical reasons. Offering no reason drops your success rate by more than a third. A "good" reason in this case would be a favorable comparison with what others in your position make, or a quantification of your contributions in your last job that demonstrate your real value.

Be real. "It has to be genuine, though, and you have to do it all the time," Pynchon says. "People don't like it when you're clearly out to gain something. It makes them feel hustled."

Make small concessions. "Research shows that people's satisfaction with the outcome of a negotiation is primarily tied to the number of concessions the other side makes," Pynchon says. "Set your expectations high and make small concessions, or offer to do more work for the same money, to make people happy. You're trying to build something durable, so it helps if both people come out feeling as if they've won something."

BOTTOM-LINE NEGOTIATION TACTICS

Research competitive salary information for your position, industry and region.

Calculate the total value of your last compensation package, including base, bonus, commission and any other extras. Be prepared to be specific and exhaustive.

If you're asked for salary history, ask what the company is prepared to offer.

Don't lie. Expect that the company can and will check every number.

Explain why you're worth what you're asking based on your research of the market, not your previous salary.

Title vs. Salary

IT'S ALWAYS TOUGH TO LAND A JOB WITH A TOP TITLE. Making concessions to secure one could be a mistake, however, according to career coaches. Candidates trying to land their first peak management job—one in which they have full profit-and-loss responsibility for a discrete organization—face intense competition when highly qualified people are scrambling for position. That's the advice of Roy Cohen, who holds the title "master career coach" at the Five O'Clock Club, a private outplacement and career-counseling club based in New York.

Their rarity makes prestige titles seem even more valuable to many job seekers—so valuable they may give up substantial salary or other benefits to obtain them. Big mistake, according to Lindsay Olson, partner and recruiter at Paradigm Staffing. Desperation—whether that means consenting to take any job

6 STEPS TO LEVERAGE A COUNTEROFFER FOR A LARGER SALARY

Leveraging a competitive offer can be a tricky and potentially risky affair. Follow these steps to put yourself in the best position to leverage a competitive offer for a better deal or successfully retreat, if necessary.

1. Don't bluff. If you're not prepared to take the counteroffer, don't try to leverage it to obtain a raise. Be prepared for either party to refuse to negotiate or rescind the offer.

2. Act before Day 1. Your best bet to leverage a competitive offer is during negotiations

with a potential new employer. They are already in the process of approving a salary and a range for you.

3. Evaluate yourself. If you're asking a current employer to match an offer, know whether you're overcompensated—in terms of salary, benefits and so on—and/or overperforming.

4. Consider the reaction. If you're currently employed, the company's performance and your treatment during the past 12 months should predict how your bosses will react. And

when it comes to a potential new employer, consider your treatment during the negotiation process to get a feel for their response.

5. State your demands. It's not about the money. List everything from working conditions to staff assignments that will make you happy in the new job.

6. Take it off the table. Be prepared to give up some of your demands, which will please the other party and improve your bargaining power.

that's offered or accepting an inflated title with a deflated salary—makes a candidate less appealing.

It's possible that a good title will give you better opportunities in the future—but only if the company has enough reputation that your position there can get you a commensurate job somewhere else. Titles and responsibilities vary significantly, and they are often inflated by companies that will "promote" valuable employees to higher-level titles without the salary or responsibility to match. As a result, the value of most titles has been deflated. In fact, increasing the seniority of your job title is a better tactic for a counteroffer than for an initial discussion.

How to Turn a Job Offer Into a Raise

IF THE LAST TIME YOU LOOKED FOR A JOB was before the recent recession, it can be hard to imagine employing the sort of career strategies and tactics that were common the decade before. These days few people talk about climbing the corporate ladder and holding out for more money; instead, common wisdom has focused more on lateral moves to secure companies, accepting smaller salaries and racing to snap up job offers before someone else does.

But even in a market that favors the employer, recruiters and compensation experts say HR departments are anxious to keep the employees they have and are often willing to go the extra mile to avoid needing to groom new top talent. One tactic, leveraging a larger salary offer from a competitor, remains an effective tool to promote your career and grow your income. And as the economy improves, so too should your willingness to employ this bargaining tactic.

But leveraging a competitive offer can be a tricky and potentially risky affair. You risk offending your current employer and putting your job in jeopardy; meanwhile, if the new employer views you as a mercenary, it may rescind the offer. A job seeker must know when to try it and when to back off; when she's playing a legitimate hand and when she's bluffing.

Try the new boss first

Approaching a current boss with what amounts to a threat that you'll leave is never comfortable, and it exerts only limited leverage because you're already on the payroll. You can get more mileage from a competitive offer when you're negotiating to take a new job. With a new hire, the authority who approves salaries and benefits has already signed off on a specific salary number and on a range within which that number could change, depending on the candidate, according to Jay Edelman, president of Top 5 Data Services.

"By the time you're negotiating, they've already vetted you and they have the money, and it's a lot more likely they'll say, 'If it takes another $25,000 to get this person, let's just give it to them and get on with things,' " Edelman says. "They might give it to you as a signing bonus or other one-time thing, but that's when they're going to be most open to those kinds of considerations." The key in that case is to articulate the factors that will make you happy or unhappy in a new job and use the leverage you have to structure the job in a way that will help you succeed in it. "Being in a job where you don't feel respected is intolerable, no matter what they pay you," adds Pynchon.

Approach your current company delicately

If you are going to use a third-party offer as leverage within your current company, start by considering how your employer will react. If you're approaching your current employer with a competitive offer, the company's performance and your treatment during the past 12 months should give you a clue to its response.

"Companies have been making changes in their compensation programs, not so much in salaries, but in smaller bonuses, higher thresholds to trigger a bonus, more limits on restricted stock options and other things," Edelman says.

"If you've been there more than a year and your compensation doesn't show you're on the positive side of that—more benefits, showing that the company really values you—you have to assume you're not the highest value on the team," Edelman points out. "That doesn't mean the company doesn't value you; if you're still there, it probably does. But your reception, if you go in with a competitive offer, may not be what you want."

Prepare your demands

Before you ask a current employer or future employer to entertain a competitive offer, you should sit down and figure out what exactly you're hoping to gain or change through negotiations.

What's at the top of the list? "The answer to that, by the way, is never, ever, ever, 'More money,' " Pynchon says. "More often it's a change in the associates you work with, the kinds of projects you work on or your career path. When you make a list of things to negotiate about, don't go in thinking about the money first." A list of other potential changes gives your boss things to take off the table without stopping the conversation completely.

"Every piece of research has shown that the more you give up in a negotiation, the happier your negotiating partner is," Pynchon says. "So having some things you can give up without too much pain will do a lot to help maintain that relationship." Be prepared for a conversation that may not go your way, however, and don't invest so much of your ego in the numbers that you end up declining the offer out of spite.

Finally, don't forget that if you're doing well in your current position, your security might be more valuable than an incremental increase in compensation. "It's almost always the case that you can [perform] better in a current job than a new one, anyway, so most of the time it's smarter not to take the other offer," Pynchon counsels. "But it's hard for overachievers to say 'no' to another $100,000."

Every piece of research has shown that the more you give up in a negotiation, the happier your negotiating partner will be.

CHECKLIST: SALARY NEGOTIATION

○ **Base salary:** Can you identify a competitive base salary for each job you're actually purusing?

....

○ **Know what you're worth in your area.** Have you done your research? Do you know the current market value of your position in your geography?

....

○ **Monetize what you do.** Have you demonstrated how you will make or save the company money?

....

○ **Do you reveal your income?** If you're asked to reveal your current income, are you prepared to dodge and deflect the question?

....

○ **Postpone it:** Traditionally, compensation is the last element discussed in the interview. If a company pressures you to discuss salary early, are you prepared to delay the conversation with a specific phrase?

....

○ **Want the job:** Can you be clear that you want the job, even though you want to continue negotiating the salary?

....

○ **Leverage a competitive offer:** Are you ready to leverage a competitive offer between two new employers or a new one and your current job? Don't bluff, and know when to quit before you lose either or both offers.

....

○ **Bonus and benefits:** For your target jobs, what percentage of total compensation is typically based on bonus and benefits?

....

○ **Security:** Do companies on your list frequently offer contracts?

....

○ **Moving costs:** If you're on the move for work, will the company pay for it?

....

○ **Signing bonus:** Is there one?

....

○ **Equity:** Does the company offer equity, and how much is typical?

....

○ **Is a good title worth giving up a little salary?** It's possible that a good title will give you better opportunities in the future—but only if the company has enough reputation that your position there can get you a commensurate job somewhere else.

8

PREPARE TO FEEL STUPID

FI

90 DA

LEAVE SOME OF YOUR KNOWLEDGE BEHIND

SPREAD THE WORD

FITTING IN TO NEW SURROUNDINGS

TH

RST NO
REST
BETWEEN
JOBS

YS THE
FIRST
QUESTIONS

ON YOU
SHOULD
ASK

JOB

"Hi, I'm Matthew! What's your name?"

When's the last time you were the new kid? For many folks who've worked their way up into the senior ranks, their last memories of first-day jitters may be distant indeed.

There are a couple of challenges at work for senior employees making the switch to a new company: Their expectations about workplace mores and rhythms may have slipped into a well-worn groove based on years of success, and their first days will be far more visible than those of more-junior colleagues.

One of my most rigorous new-kid moments occurred when I took over the Web site operations for a magazine company with a varied portfolio of titles. I inherited a staff of 50 in three cities, representing about 10 specialized topics and a range of functional specialties.

Before I started, I made a point of contacting the senior members of my team as well as my future colleagues to speak with them about the good, bad and ugly of the company and our department's role. And I walked straight out of the mandatory HR orientation into a conference room where I'd requested a meeting with all 30-some members of our New York team. It was a high-stress moment for me, but it also broke the ice and got me off to a running start.

The First Questions You Should Ask

YOU'VE BEEN OUT OF WORK FOR MONTHS.

You got the interview.

You nailed the interview.

You got the job.

You have to hit the ground running.

Now what?

Now ask the questions you didn't, or couldn't, ask during the interview. The ones that will help you do everything from effectively managing your budget to knowing what to wear on Fridays. It's also your chance to find out about the culture of the company at a level of detail that would have appeared presumptuous to ask during the interview phase. "The first thing I would tell people is keep it positive," says Cheryl Palmer, president of CalltoCareer.com. "For example, ask a co-worker, 'What do you like most about the boss?' Don't ask, 'What do you hate about the boss?' When you're first starting out, you want to be on good terms with everybody."

Veterans of the organization are also likely to be suspicious of newcomers digging for dirt. "Those who know the ropes don't want to be seen as being negative about the company or the boss or anything else," Palmer says. "The best thing is to keep it positive and people are more likely to want to answer your questions."

One particularly thorny issue for new hires is how to deal with internal candidates you beat for the job, some of whom you will need to work alongside or manage in the future. Kelley Rexroad, founder of KREX Consulting, a human-resources consulting firm, recommends new hires identify any internal candidates who were overlooked in the hiring process and reach out to smooth feathers they wouldn't otherwise know were ruffled.

"You want to be sensitive to their feelings and hear their ideas," she says. "The person could feel passed over, think you are making more money than they are. Without that knowledge, you may feel a cold shoulder and wonder why. You can win over the person with something like this: 'I understand that you applied for this role. What about it interested you?' Then engage him or her: What do they think will be tough to do? What do they think the priorities are, and what do they want to work on now? It may be possible to turn that person into a successor."

Lisa Quast, president and founder of Career Woman Inc. and a certified executive coach and author, recommends new hires reach out both to their new boss and new co-workers. Ask your new boss about goals and objectives but also about what keeps her up at night. "I like to find out what worries my boss the most so I can determine creative ways to help alleviate her worries, through new projects, improving processes, etc.," says Quast. "Companies look for employees who add value, so try to find creative and inspiring ways to show how much you can add."

Quast suggests that in your first weeks you take the time to ask co-workers what they are working on and how you might be able to help. "This will give you a good picture of the projects being worked on by individuals, as well as projects that are larger in scope and being worked on by many within or even outside the department," she says.

Fitting Into New Surroundings

OF COURSE, IN ADDITION TO GOALS AND OBJECTIVES, you also want to know corporate-culture stuff, like what to wear on Fridays. Linda Matias, author of *"201 Knock-out Answers to Tough Interview Questions: The Ultimate Guide to Handling the New Competency-Based Interview Style,"* suggests digging to find out what type of personality succeeds with the company.

"Every organization has its own culture," she says. "Team members with certain personalities may get noticed more often and receive promotions. Armed with this information, you can assess whether or not you will naturally excel in the company or if you have to flex your personality style."

Angie Maizlish, president of First Impressions and a certified professional resume writer and certified employment interview professional, explains that being successful in a new position requires a plan of action. This, she says, requires a list of good questions and a notebook and pen (or a BlackBerry or iPhone) to record the answers.

Some of the questions Maizlish suggests are:

What do you want me to accomplish the first week? Second? Third?
Where do you see me one month from now?
What tools do I need to be familiar with to be successful?
Do you have a mentor program?
To whom do I address questions? What is the best way to communicate?
What method of communication do you prefer?
Do you have an open-door policy, or is there a set time during which I can direct any questions?
What are the top three goals for me this quarter?
Can I eat lunch at my desk?
Where is the bathroom?

Finding the right answers to all of these questions (especially the last) will go a long way toward ensuring a smooth start in your new job.

HIT THE GROUND RUNNING

10 tasks to complete between a job offer and your first day on the job.

1. **Close the loop** with your former boss and co-workers. Provide as much notice as possible, write a thoughtful resignation letter and do as much as you can to ease the transition for the people you will be leaving behind.

2. **Don't burn any bridges.** Even if the experience at your former job was horrible, keep all communications thoughtful and dignified. It truly is a small world, and you never know what will happen in the future.

3. **After all of the preparation** you did to land the job, now is the time to do more. Request access to any and all information relating to your new position, including org charts.

4. **Get to know** the people with whom you will be working. If you can set up a time to meet with new associates before you start, that's ideal. If not, try to set up introductory meetings in advance, so that you will get to know the people you will be working with—and for—right away.

5. **Complete as much paperwork** and orientation as possible beforehand. Filling out forms and sitting through benefits videos can eat up a lot of precious time during your first days on the job. Work with your new manager and HR to get as much "HR housekeeping" done before your first day as possible.

6. **Leverage social-networking sites** such as LinkedIn and Twitter not only to announce your new role but also to collaborate with your new colleagues. In addition, sign up for any feeds from your company, its partners and its competitors.

7. **Develop a set of goals** for the first week, the first month and the first 90 days in your new position.

8. **Map your route.** Were your interviews scheduled to occur so that you had to travel during rush hour? If not, make sure you know how long it will take you to reach your destination during the most congested times of the day.

9. **Prepare to feel a little stupid.** Starting any new job is rough. Acknowledge beforehand that you won't have all of the answers your first day on the job, and be prepared to ask lots of questions.

10. **Take a (modest) breather.** The time between the job offer and the job may be busy, but things are bound to be busier once you start your new position. Be sure to allot some time to relax and regroup while you have the chance.

No Rest Between Jobs

YOU'VE CLEANED UP YOUR RESUME, worked your network, aced interviews and landed a job. Now it's time to relax and recharge before you start the grind anew in a fresh job. Right?

Not when you've reached the senior ranks.

The pace at which executives are expected to get with the corporate program leaves them little time to orient. Thus, the time between a job offer and your first day on the job is a window of opportunity to get a head start on making the job work for you. It's also a chance to tie up loose ends with your old job or your job search, manage relationships, and prepare your professional network to migrate with you to the next position.

Far from a rest-and-recuperation cycle, this stretch could be the busiest time of your life, says James Thompson, vice president of business development for JMJ Phillip, a recruiting and research firm that specializes in manufacturing and information technology.

"Like it or not, most people, regardless of the position, are under evaluation for the first few months or even longer," Thompson says. "You may have done research prior to the interviews, but you should still do as much preparation as you can prior to your start date. Everyone loves to see someone hit the ground running, and the higher you are up the ladder, the less hand-holding is going to be done."

Carol Meerschaert says the three weeks were critical between her last day at her old job and her first day as the director of marketing and communications for the Healthcare Businesswomen's Association. "You want to hit the ground running and show you know your stuff," she says.

During her three weeks between jobs, Meerschaert read everything she could get her hands on about her new organization and offered to assist in any way she could to ease her entry into the group. She even sat in on a two-hour conference call while in New York on vacation.

"I knew that a lot of people wanted this job, so to prove myself, I read the whole Web site," she says. "This sounds boring, and it is, but I wanted to get as much

DON'T LET YOUR STYLE SLIP!

Most of us begin every new job with the best intentions to dress sharp five days a week, 50 weeks a year. But alarm clocks and laundry days eventually win out, and our wardrobe weakens.

0-3 MONTHS

You lay out your outfit the night before, planning ahead depending on what the day entails. Even your most uncomfortable shoes and binding (yet sharp!) pencil skirt get worn. You never loosen your tie after lunch, and your jacket is always on. Casual Fridays mean nothing to you.

3-6 MONTHS

Still concerned with looking sharp, your look is still planned out and professional. But after lunch, your look tends to gets a little sloppy: tie loose, jacket on the back of the chair, heels under the desk.

information as I could. Also, it's a marketing and communications position, so I wanted to see what their marketing and communications were—where my work would be cut out for me."

The time between a job offer and start date can make or break your early performance and reputation at a company, say recruiters and human-resource experts who have seen candidates thrive and fail early on the job. Abby Kohut, president and staffing consultant of Staffing Symphony, advises the candidates she works with "to be particularly interested in a company's products, services, financials and culture. During the first few weeks learning about the who, what, where, why and how is the main responsibility."

That kind of due diligence makes new employees "much more productive in their first 100 days," says Tony Deblauwe, the founder of HR4Change, a resource for personal and corporate development services. Deblauwe recommends that new hires work with their managers and human-resources departments to obtain information such as org charts, talent inventories and marketing data on product strategies. This provides "a picture from the data of where they need to focus and use that information in the one-on-one meetings with key stakeholders that occur in the first 45 days," he explains. "They also figure out who to partner with to begin delegating tasks and identifying high-potential talent who are eager to move quickly."

Meerschaert was particularly interested in learning as much as she could about the people with whom she would be working, especially since she would be working remotely. In addition to communicating with her soon-to-be colleagues by e-mail

6-12 MONTHS

Mornings are harder and alarms more annoying. Since you have quit laying out your outfit the night before, you stand in your closet sleepy and usually end up wearing something quite similar to the day before. You can't bear those tight shoes anymore, so your favorite, slightly worn pair is the staple. You officially wear jeans for the first time on Friday, with a sport coat of course!

1-3 YEARS

You are on style autopilot. You wear a suit when you have to, but overall your dry-cleaning bill has been cut in half, since you don a polo whenever possible. You would much rather spend money on your golf or weekend wardrobe than your professional look. Even if it means looking a little dated and frumpy at the office—who cares! You fully embrace casual Friday, sometimes even starting on Thursday.

3+ YEARS

You haven't bought new work clothes in three years, and your assistant secretly tracks your mood based on your shirt ('cause yes, she has them all memorized). You forgot how to tie a tie, so your wife has to buy you clip-on ties for days you are required to wear one. You wear one black sock and one blue sock on a daily basis and are campaigning for casual Monday through Fridays.

and phone, Meerschaert attended in-person networking events where she got the lowdown on the people with whom she would be working and to whom she'd report.

Spread the Word

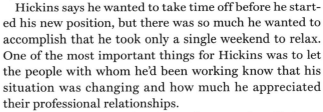

SOCIAL-NETWORKING SITES ARE ANOTHER VALUABLE TOOL to effectively bridge the gap between one job and another. After formally resigning from her previous position, Meerschaert immediately announced her new job on her LinkedIn status update, where she knew many members of the Healthcare Businesswomen's Association would read the news. Meerschaert also used her Twitter account to announce her new role. "It showed the pride I had in landing this job," she says.

Michael Hickins also used social-networking sites, including Facebook, LinkedIn and Twitter, to announce that he was taking on a new role, developing online products for *The Wall Street Journal.* Before that, Hickins had been blogging for organizations including *InformationWeek* and BNET.

Hickins says he wanted to take time off before he started his new position, but there was so much he wanted to accomplish that he took only a single weekend to relax. One of the most important things for Hickins was to let the people with whom he'd been working know that his situation was changing and how much he appreciated their professional relationships.

"What I did the first few days [after I got the offer] was reach out to everyone who had been a source," Hickins says. "I thanked each person for being a good source, for keeping me in the loop or what have you. I told them I had a great new job, that I was really happy and that I would share more details when I could." Hickins says this step was important so his clients had as much notice as possible that he was moving on to something different but also to make sure that doors would be open in the future.

"You never know what's going to happen," Hickins says. "I mean, [the offer from *The Wall Street Journal*] was as solid a job offer as you could get, but you never know. So I wanted to make sure that no one was offended because of me suddenly disappearing off the face of the planet and not doing them the courtesy of telling them what was going on."

A kind and thoughtful resignation letter as soon as you accept a new position also maintains a bridge to past relationships. Even if your experience was less than

HR HOUSEKEEPING

Before starting in your new job, try to accomplish these tasks so you won't lose valuable time in the first week:

Ask HR if you can fill out paperwork online ahead of time.

Request business cards.

Ask if technology can be ready for you on the first day.

Schedule meetings with key players for the first week.

Go in a day or two early to set up your office and briefly meet your team.

pleasant, "You may have no plans to ever return to your previous employer regardless of the situation," says JMJ Phillip's Thompson. "But in five years … you never know when someone else has jumped ship [to another company] and may want to give you a call to bring you aboard with them."

There are other loose ends to tie up, such as passing the torch of institutional knowledge and ensuring a smooth procedural transition. These were important to Meerschaert as she prepared to exit her former job. She spent time letting the vendors she had been working with know she was leaving. She also worked diligently to ease the transition for her soon-to-be-former co-workers, especially since the manager there had recently left the organization and the department was shrinking.

Meerschaert and her former employer were aided by the fact that she had long operated under a philosophy she called her "hit-by-a-bus attitude." "Tomorrow, you could get hit by a bus," she says. "Can somebody come in and do your job?" This mindset drove Meerschaert to keep exacting records of processes and procedures that she was able to pass on to co-workers to enable a smooth transition.

Prepare to Feel Stupid

THE LOSS OF A JOB is widely considered to be one of life's most stressful events, but so is the start of a new job. Going from being the go-to person when questions need answering to being the person who needs to ask all of the questions is difficult, to say the least. It's important to acknowledge this as you make your transition. "Do not expect to move mountains during your first week," says Kohut.

Hickins went so far as to rehearse the emotions of that first day. "I spent some time thinking about my past experiences with a new job, where the first couple of weeks [were] really hard emotionally," he remembers. "I'd come home and feel like, 'I really don't know if I can do this—maybe it's beyond me, maybe I got a job that's too hard for me.'"

Hickins says this process helped him set realistic expectations for himself so he "didn't feel like a failure because I hadn't solved all of the world's problems on my first day of the job." Meerschaert agrees. "You just know that you're going to go in and you're going to feel stupid for a while because you don't know what's going on."

Nevertheless, she says, it's important to remember the skill, knowledge and acumen that got you the job in the first place. "You should tread lightly and make every attempt to fit into the team and blend in with the culture," she says. "Everyone has their eyes on you, so while you should try to make a fast impact, many people and organizations find it difficult to accept change. The time will come for you to let your opinions be known, and you will sense when that is."

CHECKLIST: FIRST 90 DAYS ON THE JOB

BEFORE YOUR FIRST DAY

○ **Close the loop with your former boss and co-workers.** Provide as much notice as possible, write a thoughtful resignation letter, and do as much as you can to ease the transition for the people you will be leaving behind.

○ **Don't burn any bridges.** Even if the experience at your former job was horrible, keep all communications thoughtful and dignified. It truly is a small world, and you never know what will happen in the future.

○ **After all of the preparation you did to land the job, now is the time to do more.** Request access to any and all information relating to your new position, including org charts.

○ **Get to know the people with whom you will be working.** If you can set up a time to meet with new associates before you start, that's ideal. If not, try to set up introductory meetings in advance, so that you will get to know the people you will be working with—and for—right away.

○ **Complete as much paperwork and orientation as possible beforehand.** Filling out forms and sitting through benefits videos can eat up a lot of precious time during your first days on the job. Work with your new manager and HR to get as much "HR housekeeping" done before your first day as possible.

○ **Develop a set of goals for the first week,** the first month and the first 90 days in your new position.

○ **Map your route.** Were your interviews scheduled to occur so that you had to travel during rush hour? If not, make sure you know how long it will take you to reach your destination during the most congested times of the day.

○ **Prepare to feel a little stupid.** Starting any new job is rough. Acknowledge beforehand that you won't have all of the answers your first day on the job, and be prepared to ask lots of questions.

YOUR FIRST WEEK

○ **Break bread with colleagues.** A lot of critical information about the company will not be found in annual reports or monthly newsletters. In order to understand the unofficial rules, company politics and corporate culture, you need to have ongoing conversations with both managers and staff.

○ **Crack the company code.** When you begin a job at a new company, it can sometimes feel like you've just moved to a foreign country. Many companies have their own acronyms, lingo and inside jokes. Try to buddy up with someone who can act as a translator to get you up to speed quickly.

○ **Showcase your strengths.** You talked about your strengths during the interview process and leveraged past stories of success to prove your value-add. Take charge of a project you know you can deliver on, and then make sure that you do.

○ **Document your accomplishments.** It's never too early to start documenting job successes. One year from now, when it is time for your performance review, you want to be able to cite your accomplishments throughout the year, including those you achieved within your first critical 100 days.

○ **Find a mentor.** Connect with someone who is more senior than you and has a lengthy tenure at the company. A mentor can help you manage your career by putting you in front of the right people and exposing you to the right resources.

○ **Dress the part.** Don't put away your interview suit just yet. Observe the dress code around you, but remember, you may still be scrutinized more closely than your colleagues. Play it safe and always choose an appropriate but possibly more conservative style.

QUESTIONS TO ASK OF YOUR NEW SUPERVISORS AND CO-WORKERS

○ What do you want me to accomplish the first week? Second? Third?

○ Where do you see me one month from now?

○ What tools do I need to be familiar with to be successful?

○ To whom do I address questions? What is the best way to communicate those questions?

○ What method of communication do you prefer? Do you have an open-door policy, or is there a set time during which I can direct any questions?

○ What are the top three goals for me this quarter?

○ Can I eat at my desk?

○ Where is the bathroom?

About TheLadders

PERHAPS ONE OF THE JOB MARKET'S BIGGEST CHALLENGES: The more successful you become, the harder it is to find solid information about new job opportunities. Historically, hiring managers and recruiters don't broadcast $100K+ jobs on Web sites aimed at a wide audience for fear they'll be bombarded with resumes from unqualified candidates.

In 2003, TheLadders set out to make finding a professional job a lot easier and transformed the way $100K+ candidates connect with employers and recruiters. The solution? TheLadders created an exclusive online community charging a monthly subscription fee for full access to job listings and recruiter connections. The fee discourages those who aren't qualified from applying. To ensure that members have the right education, experience and industry expertise, TheLadders uses a two-step screening process by which every resume is reviewed twice to ensure each subscriber meets the requirements of a $100K+ candidate. When employers increase their efficiency and hire the right person for the job—everybody wins.

Today, TheLadders has grown to 4 million members, delivering pre-screened $100K+ job opportunities across all industries and locations, focused primarily on vice president, director and manager positions. TheLadders also helps job seekers and recruiters network outside traditional job listings to find unadvertised opportunities and make valuable connections. Additionally, TheLadders offers an executive-level resume-writing service and career-advice center. So whether you're headed for the corner office, you'd like to switch careers or you simply want more job satisfaction, TheLadders can help get you there.

If you're an employer or recruiter, TheLadders enables you to make business-critical hires more effectively than ever before. Employers and recruiters can post jobs; search our database of pre-screened candidates; and network with a high-quality, engaged and responsive talent pool. According to an independent survey of recruiters focusing on $100K+ talent, TheLadders ranked No. 1 for overall satisfaction when compared to all major online competitors.

TheLadders has received numerous industry awards and accolades, including Best Employment Website (2009, Webby Awards), Best Companies to Work for in New York (2009), Top 25 Most Valuable Digital Start-Ups (2009, Silicon Alley Insider), among others. In 2010, TheLadders was awarded the Corporate Community Impact Award by StreetWise Partners, which recognized the company's volunteerism to help low-income adults and youth secure good jobs and achieve economic mobility.

Come check us out on TheLadders.com.

INDEX

About the Authors

MARC CENEDELLA is Founder and CEO of TheLadders. His passion in life is jobs, their sociology and culture: the process by which everyone passes from family through school and into a career. The subject of jobs itself is Marc's chosen devotion in his professional life. Marc is a widely recognized thought leader on job search, career management, recruiting and employment-related issues. Prior to founding TheLadders, Marc was a senior vice president at HotJobs. Marc holds an MBA with high distinction from Harvard Business School, where he was named a Baker Scholar.

MATTHEW ROTHENBERG is Editor-in-Chief of TheLadders. He has written professionally about people's careers, lives and passions for more than two decades. He began his career in technology journalism and was editor-in-chief of eWEEK magazine along with stints at ZDNet, CNET and Hachette Filipacchi. Matthew won the Jesse H. Neal Award for business journalism and lives in New Jersey with his wife and children.